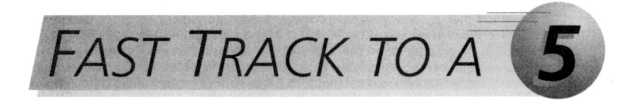

FAST TRACK TO A 5

Preparing for the **AP***
English Literature and Composition Examination

To accompany
Perrine's Literature: Structure, Sound, and Sense
by Thomas R. Arp and Greg Johnson

Angelia C. Greiner
Arkansas School for Math, Science, and the Arts, University of Arkansas

Skip Nicholson
South Pasadena High School, South Pasadena, California

 WADSWORTH
CENGAGE Learning‍

Australia • Brazil • Japan • Korea • Mexico • Singapore • Spain • United Kingdom • United States

*AP and Advanced Placement Program are registered trademarks of the College Entrance Examination
Board, which was not involved in the production of, and does not endorse, this product.

For product information and technology assistance, contact us at
**Cengage Learning Customer & Sales Support,
1-800-354-9706**

For permission to use material from this text or product, submit all requests online at **www.cengage.com/permissions**
Further permissions questions can be emailed to
permissionrequest@cengage.com

ISBN-13: 978-1-439-08227-0
ISBN-10: 1-439-08227-8

Wadsworth
20 Channel Center Street
Boston, MA 02210
USA

Cengage Learning is a leading provider of customized learning solutions with office locations around the globe, including Singapore, the United Kingdom, Australia, Mexico, Brazil, and Japan. Locate your local office at: **www.cengage.com/global**

Cengage Learning products are represented in Canada by Nelson Education, Ltd.

To learn more about Wadsworth, visit
www.cengage.com/wadsworth

Purchase any of our products at your local college store or at our preferred online store
www.ichapters.com

Credits appear on pages 180–181.

Printed in the United States of America
2 3 4 5 6 7 13 12 11 10

Part I

Strategies for the AP Exam

PREPARING FOR THE AP* EXAM

Advanced Placement courses can be both challenging and stimulating. The rigor of an AP course, whether you are taking it at your high school or through distance education, will help you prepare for the challenges of college course work. AP English Literature and Composition focuses on two skills: critical and analytical reading and clear and coherent writing about what you have read. Unlike AP Language and Composition, which concentrates on nonfiction, AP Literature and Composition draws on imaginative literature for its texts. As you explore the expanse and variety of literature, you will develop close reading skills that enable you to see how writers of literature use structure and style, along with figurative language, imagery, symbolism, and tone, to convey meaning.

The AP English Literature and Composition exam is also a writing exam in that it tests your ability to write clearly and coherently about the details and meaning of a poetry or prose selection. It is in the essay portion of the exam that you can show off your skills as a writer. When scoring essays, readers look for variety in sentence structure, sophisticated vocabulary, logical organization of ideas, and balance between the general meaning of the selection and the specific elements by which the overall meaning is developed. Don't think of the exam as something designed to trip you up; it is an opportunity to demonstrate how well you have honed your reading and writing skills.

WHAT'S IN THIS BOOK

This *Fast Track to a 5* is keyed to *Perrine's Literature: Structure, Sound, and Sense* by Thomas R. Arp and Greg Johnson, from which many of the selections are drawn. However, it is compatible with any textbook used for an AP literature course. It is designed to familiarize you with the structure of the exam and provide you with information on how to approach the test. Because a solid understanding of literary terms is indispensable for the multiple-choice questions, a glossary is included for you. Knowing these terms is important, but being able to dig deep into a selection to discern its meaning is even more important. You will find in this book a section on developing close analytical reading skills. A discussion on annotation and an annotated passage are included to help you prepare for reading the selections on the exam. Knowing how to annotate is essential, but to become truly good at it you need to make a habit of annotation. Every time you read, annotation is a must for developing close reading skills. You will also find information designed to help you prepare for writing the essays called for in Section II of the exam. There are sample prompts you can use for

---

*AP and Advanced Placement Program are registered trademarks of the College Board, which was not involved in the production of and does not endorse this product.

practice in organizing and writing the essays, as well as suggestions for creating the sophisticated writing that earns high scores.

At the end of this section you will find a diagnostic test. With fifty-five multiple-choice questions and three essay questions, it has all the components of the AP exam. Take the diagnostic test and then score it, paying special attention to the explanations provided for each multiple-choice question and the general scoring guidelines for each of the essay prompts. Your diagnostic test will give you an idea about your current abilities and help you identify which skills you have mastered and which you want to work on.

Part II of this book focuses on test preparation. It begins with a section on tone and mood, then presents the terminology that you will need for an analysis of literature. You will find yourself returning to this section often.

The next chapter looks at ways to develop close reading skills, provides an example of an annotation, and includes strategies for managing the multiple-choice test questions. The score on the multiple-choice section accounts for 45 percent of the exam grade, so you will want to have a firm understanding of how to approach those questions.

The second section of the AP exam is made up of three essay questions. The first is based on a poetry selection; the second is based on a prose selection. The final essay question, which concerns a theme, calls on you to write an essay based on a literary work of your choice. The third, fourth, and fifth chapters in Part II of this book offer tips on how to analyze poetry and prose passages for their meaning, how to determine what to include—and what to leave out—when writing your essays, and how to isolate and discuss theme.

Part III has two complete practice tests. These will give you the opportunity to practice both answering questions and managing your time on the test. The importance of practice, practice, practice cannot be stressed enough. The more familiar you are with the structure of the exam, the types of questions you will be asked, and the management of your time, the more likely you are to score well on the exam.

BEFORE THE AP EXAM

All of the books in the *Fast Track to a 5* series are designed for students to use on their own. If you have been steadily doing your homework and keeping up with the course work, you should be in good shape. The key to preparing for the AP exam is to begin early, and the first step is to set up a schedule for yourself. Take the diagnostic test to see where you are and what you want to accomplish. You may be surprised at how much material you can cover by studying thirty minutes a day for a month or so before the test. Use the practice tests to build your confidence.

The evening before the exam is not the time to cram. If you'd like, briefly review the terminology or take a quick look through class notes or your textbook, but avoid getting caught up in small details. Do get a good night's sleep. And on the day of the examination, be sure to eat breakfast—fuel for the brain. Then go get a 5.

Bring a form of identification (usually your driver's license or school ID card is sufficient). In addition, you should have two well-sharpened pencils with erasers and a dark-blue or black pen. Wear comfortable clothes. We recommend layering your clothing in case the heat or air-conditioning is erratic. There is nothing worse than roasting or freezing while you are trying to concentrate on writing! It's a good idea to wear a watch so you can keep track of the time. Letting go of your cell phone can be like saying goodbye to a best friend, but often they are not permitted in the testing room. You may be allowed to have a capped bottle of water with you, but don't assume anything! Ask first.

Once you are in your seat, the proctor will take attendance, check IDs if that hasn't already been done, and give general directions. He or she will then pass out a test booklet and read through the directions on filling out the answer sheet. When the proctor says "Begin," you will have sixty minutes to complete Section I, the fifty-five multiple-choice questions. The proctor should give a warning five minutes before your hour is up.

You will be allowed a ten-minute bathroom and water break after the multiple-choice section. This is the time to drink regular water to maintain your focus—don't overdo it or you may find yourself needing an additional and time-consuming trip to the bathroom! Think natural foods when it comes to snacks. For a quick bit of energy, bananas and apples are a much better pick than donuts. If possible, get some fresh air and stretch! Yes, all of this in just ten minutes!

Once you are back at your seat, the proctor will hand out a green booklet and a pink booklet. The green booklet will have three essay questions in it. You can make annotations in the booklet. The pink booklet has lined pages for writing your essays. Each page in the pink booklet has a box in the upper right-hand corner where you should indicate which essay question—1, 2, or 3—you are answering. You don't have to write the essays in any particular order. If you forget to put the essay number in the box, don't worry. AP readers are trained to leave no page unturned in a student test booklet. They will read all the pages in the booklet in order to find your essay. You will not be penalized for that error.

There are three essay questions on the AP exam. The first is based on poetry; the second is based on a prose or drama passage; the third asks you to respond to a general statement or question about literature, making reference to a work of your own choosing. You have two hours to work on the three essay questions. All are of the same value, so it is suggested that you spend equal time—forty minutes—on each.

Writing the three essays will feel like a purging of your brain cells! It is in this section that many students begin to panic. If you feel that happening, resist it. The key to this portion of the test is managing your time. You may find yourself spending much more time on one of the essays than on the others. Rather than leaving the third essay blank and polishing the second essay to try to attain a higher score, it's better to stop where you are and focus on a response to the third essay prompt. Why? Even if you were able to raise the score on the second essay by a point, you would lose valuable time for your third essay, costing you much more than a single point. AP readers know that you don't have enough time to "polish" an essay. When you complete an

Taking the AP English Literature and Composition Exam

The purpose of the Advanced Placement program hasn't changed since 1955, when it was first introduced: It was designed to give students an opportunity to extend their knowledge with meaningful and engaging college-level course work. Year in and year out, the number of students taking AP courses continues to grow—more than 298,000 students took the AP English Literature and Composition exam in 2008! Students value the abilities to read critically, to make insightful connections between what they read and the larger world, and to write cogently about ideas. Those abilities enrich the individual. They are also the foundation for a free-thinking society.

About the Exam

If you are enrolled in an English Literature and Composition (or English IV AP) course, you are being given a year's instruction in the skills necessary for success on the AP exam. Most students who take the class will take the test—many took the AP English Language and Composition exam the year before. Some schools require students in AP classes to take the exam. Keep in mind that a formal year-long course is not a necessity. Any high school student may take any AP examination. Our advice to students in an AP course is always to take the test. Even if you don't get a high grade, you will have grown as a thinker and a writer. AP makes you far better prepared for college courses.

To take the test, you need to sign up with your school counselor or the designated AP coordinator at your high school campus. Each test costs approximately $86. However, please note that many states and districts offer a variety of financial incentives for taking the tests, so you may not be charged the full amount.

The AP exams are given during May on high school campuses worldwide. The methods of scoring and grading will be discussed in detail later, but for now just know that the exams are scored in June by AP teachers and college professors. Students receive their grades in the middle of July. You can have the College Board send your grades directly to the colleges of your choice. If you are not yet ready to apply to a college, you can have your grades "banked," to be sent at a later date.

Examination Day

The AP English Literature and Composition exam is nearly always given in the morning and lasts approximately three and half hours.

mourners drifted in till the pub was half full.

"Dadda," I said, pulling his coat again, "can't we go home now?"

"Ah, your mother won't be in for a long time yet," he said benevolently enough. "Run out in the road and play, can't you."

It struck me very cool, the way grown-ups assumed that you could 25
play all by yourself on a strange road. I began to get bored as I had so often been bored before. I knew Father was quite capable of lingering there till nightfall. I knew I might have to bring him home, blind drunk, down Blarney Lane, with all the old women at their doors, saying: "Mick Delaney is on it again." I knew that my mother would be half 30
crazy with anxiety; that next day Father wouldn't go out to work; and before the end of the week she would be running down to the pawn with the clock under her shawl. I could never get over the lonesomeness of the kitchen without a clock.

I was still thirsty. I found if I stood on tiptoe I could just reach 35
Father's glass, and the idea occurred to me that it would be interesting to know what the contents were like. He had his back to it and wouldn't notice. I took down the glass and sipped cautiously. It was a terrible disappointment. I was astonished that he could even drink such stuff. It looked as if he had never tried lemonade. 40

12. It can be inferred from the passage that the boy and his father are
   (A) returning from a funeral
   (B) on their way to a wedding
   (C) shopping for the boy's ill mother
   (D) out for a father-and-son day together
   (E) trying to avoid going to work and to school

13. When the boy says, "[I]f I was to act as a brake" (line 5), he means if he were to
   (A) invent a game to play in the road
   (B) stop the carriages from leaving
   (C) keep the "shawly women" from leaving
   (D) help his father avoid going "out to work" (line 31)
   (E) prevent his father from drinking

14. The "consolation" the men brought to the "mysterious females" (lines 2–3) was most likely
   (A) notes of condolence from well-wishers
   (B) glasses of beer
   (C) soothing physical contact meant to reassure
   (D) the welcome news that their journey was almost over
   (E) shawls to keep them warm

15. The effect of limiting the boy's dialogue to the repetition of the same sentence is to
   (A) contrast with the observations of "the old women" in line 29
   (B) foreshadow the boy's tasting the pint
   (C) serve as a balance for the sadness of the "men in black ties"
   (D) emphasize the boy's discomfort
   (E) imply mild disapproval of the boy's inability to amuse himself

16. The father is characterized chiefly by
   (A) his treatment of the "mysterious females" (line 3)
   (B) what the author has him say
   (C) the old women's disapproval of him
   (D) his style of dress
   (E) the boy's account of his actions

GO ON TO THE NEXT PAGE

17. In this passage, the narrator's chief purpose is best described as
    (A) giving a detailed account of his introduction to strong drink
    (B) satirizing his own youthful foolishness
    (C) revealing the reasons for his intense dislike of his father
    (D) evaluating his introduction to adulthood
    (E) meditating on the variety of reactions from different characters to a simple incident

18. Which of the following phrases most closely describes the father's actions in lines 12–21?
    (A) "affliction's sons are brothers in distress" —Robert Burns
    (B) "sweet reluctant amorous delay" —John Milton
    (C) "Drink not the third glass, which thou canst not tame"—George Herbert
    (D) "always vulgar and often convincing" —Oscar Wilde
    (E) "divinely bent on meditation" —William Shakespeare

19. Which of the following patterns of syntax best characterizes the pervading style of the passage?
    (A) sentences with heavy subordination and complexity
    (B) a steady progression from simple to highly complex sentences
    (C) a combination of simple sentences and questions
    (D) rhetorical questions mixed with short, contrasting declarations
    (E) early sentences heavy with narrative giving way to straightforward explanation

20. The narrator's statement "I took down the glass and sipped cautiously" (line 38) is ironic when seen in relation to the phrase
    (A) "It was a terrible disappointment" (lines 38–39)
    (B) "I was still thirsty" (line 35)
    (C) "I began to get bored" (line 26)
    (D) "it would be interesting to know what the contents were like" (line 37)
    (E) "I was to act as a brake" (line 5)

21. Of the following, the scene or incident LEAST intended to have a humorous intent is
    (A) the father's sending the boy out into the road to play
    (B) the "mysterious females" reaching out of their carriages
    (C) the father preparing his pipe
    (D) the kitchen "without a clock"
    (E) the boy's reaction to his first taste of the pint

22. The narrator's overall tone in the passage is best described as one of
    (A) pedantic reproach
    (B) somber regret
    (C) amused reflection
    (D) effusive euphoria
    (E) ominous serenity

QUESTIONS 23–33. Carefully read the poem by Sylvia Plath before choosing your answers.

Mirror

I am silver and exact. I have no preconceptions.
Whatever I see I swallow immediately
Just as it is, unmisted by love or dislike.
I am not cruel, only truthful—
The eye of a little god, four-cornered.   5
Most of the time I meditate on the opposite wall.
It is pink, with speckles. I have looked at it so long
I think it is a part of my heart. But it flickers.
Faces and darkness separate us over and over.

Now I am a lake. A woman bends over me,   10
Searching my reaches for what she really is.
Then she turns to those liars, the candles or the moon.
I see her back, and reflect it faithfully.
She rewards me with tears and an agitation of hands.
I am important to her. She comes and goes.   15
Each morning it is her face that replaces the darkness.
In me she has drowned a young girl, and in me an old woman
Rises toward her day after day, like a terrible fish.

23. The poem draws its perspective primarily from the
    (A) comforting metaphor of the candles and the moon
    (B) gradual glorification of the "little god, four-cornered" (line 5)
    (C) extended personification of the mirror
    (D) illustrative allegory of the lake
    (E) ironic manipulation of light and dark images

24. The word "swallow" (line 2) is best understood to mean
    I. absorb or envelop
    II. accept without question
    III. keep from expressing or showing
    (A) I and II
    (B) I only
    (C) II only
    (D) I and III only
    (E) I, II, and III

25. The phrase "eye of a little god" (line 5) is best interpreted to imply
    (A) the mirror's devotion to its meditation (line 6)
    (B) the mirror's close relationship to "love or dislike" (line 3)
    (C) the mirror's unassailable dominance
    (D) the value of the silver (line 1)
    (E) the woman, who brings light to "the darkness" (line 16)

26. The antecedents of the pronoun "us" in line 9 are
    (A) the woman and the "candles or the moon" (line 12)
    (B) the mirror and the pink wall
    (C) humans and their emotions
    (D) the mirror and the woman
    (E) the mirror and "love or dislike" (line 3)

27. The most notable shift that separates the two stanzas is a change in
    (A) the level of abstraction, from more concrete to more abstract images
    (B) focus, from the mirror to the woman
    (C) the rhyme scheme, from regular to random
    (D) the prevailing rhythm, from irregular to iambic pentameter
    (E) syntactic complexity, from simple to complicated

28. Which of the following best restates the meaning of line 9?
    (A) People block the mirror's view of the wall, and it cannot see it in the dark.
    (B) As humans, we repeatedly see our own futures only darkly.
    (C) Love based only on physical beauty will flicker like a candle and go out.
    (D) Only art can bridge the darkness that separates people's faces.
    (E) In the mirror's vision, the speckles on the wall become faces that peer into the darkness.

29. The speaker implies that the "candles [and] the moon" are "liars" (line 12) because
    (A) they offer a light that makes the woman appear more attractive than she is
    (B) they change through phases and are undependable
    (C) they are distorted by the mirror
    (D) they are twisted by "love or dislike" (line 3) and fail to be truthful
    (E) they are only reflections in the "lake" (line 10)

GO ON TO THE NEXT PAGE

30. The poet's choice of the word "faithfully" in line 13 most directly reinforces
    (A) "meditate" (line 6)
    (B) "part of my heart" (line 8)
    (C) "unmisted" (line 3)
    (D) "cruel" (line 4)
    (E) "the candles or the moon" (line 12)

31. Taken alone, the phrase "I see her back" (line 13) suggests that the mirror does all the following EXCEPT
    (A) empathize with the woman and feel a need to reflect her "faithfully"
    (B) perceive the back of the woman's body as she turns away
    (C) escort the woman back to the world of reality
    (D) return the woman's look
    (E) understand that she has returned from "the candles or the moon"

32. "[H]er face that replaces the darkness" (line 16) refers to the
    (A) woman's turning on the light
    (B) biblical story of Eve in the Garden of Eden
    (C) "love or dislike" (line 3)
    (D) gladness the mirror feels at seeing the woman return
    (E) act of creation by the "little god" (line 5)

33. Which of the following best describes the poem as a whole?
    (A) a didactic, philosophical poem about humans and our relationship to our possessions
    (B) a satiric anecdote exposing human vanity
    (C) a lyrical demonstration of the need for love to make life significant
    (D) a poignant meditation on the consolations of nature
    (E) a somber reflection on our perceptions of our own aging

QUESTIONS 34–44. Carefully read the passage from William Shakespeare's *Othello,* Act I, Scene 3, before choosing your answers.

> OTHELLO: Her father loved me, oft invited me,
> Still questioned me the story of my life
> From year to year, the battles, sieges, fortunes,
> That I have passed.
> I ran it through, even from my boyish days   5
> To the very moment that he bade me tell it.
> Wherein I spake of most disastrous chances,
> Of moving accidents by flood and field,
> Of hairbreadth 'scapes i' the imminent deadly breach,
> Of being taken by the insolent foe   10
> And sold to slavery, of my redemption thence,
> And portance in my travels' history.
> Wherein of antres¹ vast and deserts idle,
> Rough quarries, rocks, and hills whose heads touch heaven,
> It was my hint to speak—such was the process.   15
> And of the cannibals that each other eat,
> The anthropophagi,² and men whose heads
> Do grow beneath their shoulders. This to hear
> Would Desdemona seriously incline.
> But still the house affairs would draw her thence,   20
> Which ever as she could with haste dispatch,

---

¹ Caves.
² Cannibals.

She'd come again, and with a greedy ear
Devour up my discourse. Which I observing,
Took once a pliant hour and found good means
To draw from her a prayer of earnest heart   25
That I would all my pilgrimage dilate,
Whereof by parcels she had something heard,
But not intentively. I did consent,
And often did beguile her of her tears
When I did speak of some distressful stroke   30
That my youth suffered. My story being done,
She gave me for my pains a world of sighs.
She swore, in faith, 'twas strange, 'twas passing strange,
'Twas pitiful, 'twas wondrous pitiful.
She wished she had not heard it, yet she wished   35
That Heaven had made her such a man. She thanked me,
And bade me, if I had a friend that loved her,
I should but teach him how to tell my story
And that would woo her. Upon this hint[3] I spake.
She loved me for the dangers I had passed,   40
And I loved her that she did pity them.
This only is the witchcraft I have used.

34. From the passage it can reasonably be inferred that Othello has probably been accused of trying to win the hand of Desdemona by
   (A) lying to her father about his past
   (B) pretending he was wooing for a friend
   (C) involving himself in the slave trade
   (D) using magic
   (E) fighting battles for her

35. In the passage as a whole, Othello uses a rhetorical structure that
   (A) moves gradually from more general to more specific examples of his main idea
   (B) anticipates counterarguments and attempts to defuse them one at a time
   (C) arranges details into a narrative to support a concluding statement of his central argument
   (D) begins with an indirect statement of purpose and then arranges details in order of decreasing importance
   (E) presents an expository argument that works from abstract generalization to specific detail

36. The word "thence" (lines 11 and 20) is best understood to mean
   (A) (away) from here
   (B) (away) from there
   (C) to here
   (D) to there
   (E) to where?

37. The lines "I would all my pilgrimage dilate, / Whereof by parcels she had something heard, / But not intentively" (lines 26–28) are best paraphrased as
   (A) I would exaggerate the stories of my travels, which she had heard a little—but not much—about
   (B) I would tell her of my travels, which people had told her about, but she would not listen with any attention
   (C) I would tell her of my travels, which she had heard of in bits and pieces but not altogether
   (D) I would tell her again of my travels, repeating what I had sent in letters that included little detail
   (E) I would tell her of my travels but leaving out the parts that would offend or distress her

---

[3] Opportunity.

GO ON TO THE NEXT PAGE

38. In context, the word "passing" in line 33 has the meaning of
    (A) acceptably, moderately
    (B) extremely, surpassingly
    (C) only barely
    (D) not at all
    (E) dying

39. According to lines 33–36, Desdemona's reaction to Othello's stories is that she
    (A) felt shame and embarrassment in front of a military man who seemed so distant
    (B) wished her father could see Othello as she does
    (C) wished men like Othello could live longer lives before going to heaven so they could inspire others on Earth
    (D) hoped heaven would protect her and those she loved from creatures such as the cannibals
    (E) wished she herself could have been made such an adventurous and courageous person

40. Which two lines come closest to stating the same idea?
    (A) Lines 14 and 25
    (B) Lines 32 and 40
    (C) Lines 20 and 42
    (D) Lines 34 and 41
    (E) Lines 11 and 34

41. The first section of the passage (lines 1–18) differs from the second section (lines 18–42) in all of the following EXCEPT
    (A) sentence length
    (B) number of sentences
    (C) tone
    (D) level of abstraction
    (E) the focus of their content

42. In the context of the passage, both Desdemona and her father
    (A) repay Othello with lavish rewards
    (B) enjoy the stories Othello tells but suspect they are exaggerated
    (C) try to get away from Othello to attend to "house-affairs"
    (D) press Othello to tell the stories of his adventures
    (E) prefer the military accounts of the "battles, sieges, fortunes" to the less believable stories of cannibals and monsters

43. The line in which the poet introduces NO variety into the passage's iambic rhythm is
    (A) line 4
    (B) line 6
    (C) line 22
    (D) line 23
    (E) line 36

44. The prevailing tone of the passage taken as a whole is best characterized as
    (A) impulsively blunt and forceful
    (B) playfully pedantic and sardonic
    (C) confidently assertive and candid
    (D) aggressively supercilious and disdainful
    (E) unassumingly reticent and self-effacing

Questions 45–55. Carefully read the passage from the short story "Sonny's Blues" by James Baldwin before choosing your answers.

All I know about music is that not many people ever really hear it. And even then, on the rare occasions when something opens within, and the music enters, what we mainly hear, or hear corroborated, are personal, private, vanishing evocations. But the man who creates the music is hearing something else, is dealing with the roar rising from the void and imposing order on it as it hits the air. What is evoked in him, then, is of another order, more terrible because it has no words, and triumphant, too, for that same reason. And his triumph, when he triumphs, is ours. I just watched Sonny's face. His face was troubled, he was working hard, but he wasn't with it. And I had the feeling that, in a way, everyone on the bandstand was waiting for him, both waiting for him and pushing him along. But as I began to watch Creole, I realized that it was Creole who held them all back. He had them on a short rein. Up there, keeping the heat with his whole body, wailing on the fiddle, with his eyes half closed, he was listening to everything, but he was listening to Sonny. He was having a dialogue with Sonny. He wanted Sonny to leave the shoreline and strike out for the deep water. He was Sonny's witness that deep water and drowning were not the same thing—he had been there, and he knew. And he wanted Sonny to know. He was waiting for Sonny to do the things on the keys which would let Creole know that Sonny was in the water.

And, while Creole listened, Sonny moved, deep within, exactly like someone in torment. I had never before thought of how awful the relationship must be between the musician and his instrument. He has to fill it, this instrument, with the breath of life, his own. He has to make it do what he wants it to do. And a piano is just a piano. It's made out of so much wood and wires and little hammers and big ones, and Ivory. While there's only so much you can do with it, the only way to find this out is to try, to try and make it do everything.

And Sonny hadn't been near a piano for over a year. And he wasn't on much better terms with his life, nor the life that stretched before him now. He and the piano stammered, started one way, got scared, stopped, started another way, panicked, marked time, started again, then seemed to have found a direction, panicked again, got stuck. And the face I saw on Sonny I'd never seen before. Everything had been burned out of it, and, at the same time, things usually hidden were being burned in, by the fire and fury of the battle which was occurring in him up there.

Yet, watching Creole's face as they neared the end of the first set, I had the feeling that something had happened, something I hadn't heard. Then they finished, there was scattered applause, and then, without an instant's warning, Creole started into something else, it was almost sardonic, it was *Am I Blue*.[4] And, as though he commanded, Sonny began to play. Something began to happen. And Creole let out the reins. The dry, low, black man said something awful on the drums, Creole answered, and the drums talked back. Then the horn insisted, sweet and high, slightly detached and calm and old.

5

10

15

20

25

30

35

40

45

---

[4] A 1929 jazz standard introduced by Ethel Waters and recorded hundreds of times since then.

GO ON TO THE NEXT PAGE

Then they all came together again, and Sonny was part of the family again. I could tell this from his face. He seemed to have found, right there beneath his fingers, a damn brand-new piano. It seemed that he couldn't get over it. Then, for a while, just being happy with Sonny, they seemed to be agreeing with him that brand-new pianos certainly were a gas. 50

Then Creole stepped forward to remind them that what they were playing was the blues. He hit something in all of them, he hit something in me, myself, and the music tightened and deepened, apprehension began to beat the air. Creole began to tell us what the blues were all about. They were not about anything very new. He and his boys up there were keeping it new, at the risk of ruin, destruction, madness, and death, in order to find new ways to make us listen. For, while the tale of how we suffer, and how we are delighted, and how we may triumph is never new, it always must be heard. There isn't any other tale to tell, it's the only light we've got in all this darkness. 55 60

45. The clause "what we mainly hear, or hear corroborated, are personal, private, vanishing evocations" (lines 3–4) is best taken to mean that
(A) there is no "wrong way" to hear music
(B) we all have the potential to call up a power to help us create
(C) music calls up in us our own individual thoughts and memories
(D) our personal and immediate thoughts are usually contradicted by the music we hear
(E) nonmusicians actually hear music much as its creators do

46. The effect of the phrase "the man who creates the music" (lines 4–5) is most strongly reinforced by the phrase
(A) "the breath of life" (line 26)
(B) "the fire and fury" (line 38)
(C) "he couldn't get over it" (lines 51–52)
(D) "it has no words" (line 7)
(E) "Creole let out the reins" (line 46)

47. The narrator implies that Creole "held them all back" (line 13)
(A) to wait for inspiration to strike him
(B) to assert his leadership
(C) to give Sonny the chance to engage with the music
(D) to let the listeners catch up with the group
(E) to help the narrator understand the music

48. The phrase "in the water" (lines 21–22) is best read as a metaphor that implies
(A) Sonny's following Creole's direction
(B) Sonny's starting to find his way with improvisation
(C) Sonny's getting into difficulty he will not be able to get out of
(D) Creole's indifference at that point to Sonny's playing
(E) Sonny's blending into the group rather than sounding like a soloist

49. In lines 17–18 the author refers to the "the shoreline" and "the deep water"
(A) to stress the danger of the group's not pleasing the audience
(B) to heighten the contrast between Sonny's hesitation and his complete engagement with the music
(C) to contrast Sonny's mediocre talent with his intense performance
(D) as metaphors for the creation of a piano from wood, wire, and ivory
(E) as evidence of Creole's tight hold on the group's music

50. In the sentence "He and the piano stammered, started one way, got scared, stopped, started another way, panicked, marked time, started again, then seemed to have found a direction, panicked again, got stuck" (lines 33–36), the meaning is unmistakably reinforced by
    I. the consonant sounds
    II. the imagery
    III. the syntax
    (A) I only
    (B) I and II only
    (C) II only
    (D) II and III only
    (E) I and III only

51. The repetition of the word "something" (lines 41–46) suggests
    (A) the inadequacy of words to convey completely the experience of music
    (B) the narrator's inability to understand the musicians
    (C) the unimportance of the small details of the music
    (D) Creole's powerlessness to lead the group without Sonny's participation
    (E) the narrator's embarrassment at the weak performance

52. In the phrase "they seemed to be agreeing with him that brand-new pianos certainly were a gas" (lines 53–54), the narrator is suggesting that
    (A) they became aware that Sonny did not know how well he could play when he had only old pianos to use
    (B) they were happy that Sonny's gratitude for Creole's buying him a new piano began to show in his playing
    (C) Sonny's suddenly inspired playing aroused and excited the whole group
    (D) they recognized that the "brand-new piano" was also a curse because it came with a heavy cost
    (E) the narrator disapproved of the other musicians being happy when the credit for the improved music belonged rightly to Sonny

53. In the sentence "Then Creole stepped forward to remind them that what they were playing was the blues" (lines 55–56), the narrator is doing which of the following?
    (A) explaining why Creole takes on the role of a soloist and relegates the rest of the group to "playing backup"
    (B) justifying Creole's stopping the music so he can talk to the group about the meaning of what they are playing
    (C) disapproving of Creole's hitting out at the group and making them apprehensive about their music
    (D) despairing of the group's ability to use music to overcome "ruin, destruction, madness, and death" (lines 60–61)
    (E) rebuking Sonny for his unsuitable exuberance by shifting the narrative focus to Creole

54. The tone of the closing sentences of the passage is best described as one of
    (A) muted but insistent affirmation
    (B) frustrated but affectionate nostalgia
    (C) bleak but and anguished despair
    (D) amusing but mocking apprehension
    (E) objective and analytical detachment

55. Taken as a whole, the passage is best characterized as
    (A) a technical description of the importance of improvisation in jazz
    (B) an argument developed through the use of alternating description and exposition
    (C) a performance critique enlarged through both abstract and concrete comparison and contrast
    (D) an expository passage chiefly concerned with establishing and extending a definition
    (E) a narration that builds to an abstract statement of artistic philosophy

STOP
END OF SECTION I

Section II: Essay Questions
Number of questions: 3
Reading time: 15 minutes
Writing time: 2 hours
Suggested time for each essay: 40 minutes

Section II of this examination requires answers in essay form. Each question counts for one-third of the total essay section score. The two hours are yours to divide among the three essay questions as you think best. To help you use your time well, the proctor may announce the time at which each question should be completed. If you finish any question before time is announced, you may go on to another question. You may go back at any time and work on any essay question you want.

Each essay will be judged on its clarity and effectiveness in dealing with the assigned topic and on the quality of the writing. In response to Question 3, select a work of recognized literary merit appropriate to the question. A good general rule is to use works of the same quality as those you studied in your Advanced Placement literature course(s).

After completing each question, you should check your essay for accuracy of punctuation, spelling, and diction; you are advised, however, not to attempt many longer corrections. Remember that quality is far more important than quantity.

Write your essays clearly and legibly in dark-blue or black ink. Cross out any errors you make.

Question 1

In each of the following poems, the speaker questions God, each from a different place and time—England around 1655 in the first poem, Harlem in 1925 in the second. Carefully read each poem. Then write an essay in which you compare and contrast the two poems and analyze the relationship between them.

On His Blindness
by John Milton

When I consider how my light is spent
    Ere half my days in this dark world and wide,
    And that one talent which is death to hide
    Lodged with me useless, though my soul more bent
To serve therewith my Maker, and present   5
    My true account, lest he returning chide,
    "Doth God exact day-labor, light denied?"
    I fondly ask. But Patience, to prevent
That murmur, soon replies, "God doth not need
    Either man's work or his own gifts. Who best   10
    Bear his mild yoke, they serve him best. His state
Is kingly: thousands at his bidding speed,
    And post o'er land and ocean without rest;
    They also serve who only stand and wait."

Yet Do I Marvel
by Countee Cullen

I doubt not God is good, well-meaning, kind,
And did He stoop to quibble could tell why
The little buried mole continues blind,
Why flesh that mirrors Him must some day die,
Make plain the reason tortured Tantalus   5
Is baited by the fickle fruit, declare
If merely brute caprice dooms Sisyphus
To struggle up a never-ending stair.
Inscrutable His ways are, and immune
To catechism by a mind too strewn   10
With petty cares to slightly understand
What awful brain compels His awful hand.
Yet do I marvel at this curious thing:
To make a poet black and bid him sing!

GO ON TO THE NEXT PAGE

Question 2

The following passage is from near the opening of "Interpreter of Maladies," a short story by Jhumpa Lahiri. Carefully read the passage. Then write an essay in which you analyze, in specific terms, how Lahiri uses literary devices to define her characters. You might want to consider her use of such tools as description, diction, and dialogue, and others that help delineate the people in the story.

They were on their way to see the Sun Temple at Konarak. It was a dry, bright Saturday, the mid-July heat tempered by a steady ocean breeze, ideal weather for sightseeing. Ordinarily Mr. Kapasi would not have stopped so soon along the way, but less than five minutes after he'd picked up the family that morning in front of Hotel Sandy 5 Villa, the little girl had complained.

The first thing Mr. Kapasi had noticed when he saw Mr. and Mrs. Das, standing with their children under the portico of the hotel, was that they were very young, perhaps not even thirty. In addition to Tina they had two boys, Ronny and Bobby, who 10 appeared very close in age and had teeth covered in a network of flashing silver wires. The family looked Indian but dressed as foreigners did, the children in stiff, brightly colored clothing and caps with translucent visors.

Mr. Kapasi was accustomed to foreign tourists; he was assigned 15 to them regularly because he could speak English. Yesterday he had driven an elderly couple from Scotland, both with spotted faces and fluffy white hair so thin it exposed their sunburnt scalps. In comparison, the tanned, youthful faces of Mr. and Mrs. Das were all the more striking. When he'd introduced himself, Mr. Kapasi had 20 pressed his palms together in greeting, but Mr. Das squeezed hands like an American so that Mr. Kapasi felt it in his elbow. Mrs. Das, for her part, had flexed one side of her mouth, smiling dutifully at Mr. Kapasi, without displaying any interest in him. As they waited at the tea stall, Ronny, who looked like the older of the two boys, 25 clambered suddenly out of the back seat, intrigued by a goat tied to a stake in the ground.

"Don't touch it," Mr. Das said. He glanced up from his paperback tour book, which said "INDIA" in yellow letters and looked as if it had been published abroad. His voice, somehow 30 tentative and a little shrill, sounded as though it had not yet settled into maturity.

"I want to give it a piece of gum," the boy called back as he trotted ahead.

Mr. Das stepped out of the car and stretched his legs by 35 squatting briefly to the ground. A clean-shaven man, he looked exactly like a magnified version of Ronny. He had a sapphire blue visor, and was dressed in shorts, sneakers, and a T-shirt. The camera slung around his neck, with an impressive telephoto lens and numerous buttons and markings, was the only complicated 40 thing he wore. He frowned, watching as Ronny rushed toward the goat, but appeared to have no intention of intervening. "Bobby, make sure that your brother doesn't do anything stupid."

"I don't feel like it," Bobby said, not moving. He was sitting in the front seat beside Mr. Kapasi, studying a picture of the elephant 45 god taped to the glove compartment.

"No need to worry," Mr. Kapasi said. "They are quite tame." Mr. Kapasi was forty-six years old, with receding hair that had gone completely silver, but his butterscotch complexion and his unlined brow, which he treated in spare moments to dabs of lotus-oil balm, made it easy to imagine what he must have looked like at an earlier age. He wore gray trousers and a matching jacket-style shirt, tapered at the waist, with short sleeves and a large pointed collar, made of a thin but durable synthetic material. He had specified both the cut and the fabric to his tailor— it was his preferred uniform for giving tours because it did not get crushed during his long hours behind the wheel. Through the windshield he watched as Ronny circled around the goat, touched it quickly on its side, then trotted back to the car.

"You left India as a child?" Mr. Kapasi asked when Mr. Das had settled once again into the passenger seat.

"Oh, Mina and I were both born in America," Mr. Das announced with an air of sudden confidence. "Born and raised. Our parents live here now, in Assansol. They retired. We visit them every couple years." He turned to watch as the little girl ran toward the car, the wide purple bows of her sundress flopping on her narrow brown shoulders. She was holding to her chest a doll with yellow hair that looked as if it had been chopped, as a punitive measure, with a pair of dull scissors. "This is Tina's first trip to India, isn't it, Tina?"

"I don't have to go to the bathroom anymore," Tina announced.

"Where's Mina?" Mr. Das asked.

Mr. Kapasi found it strange that Mr. Das should refer to his wife by her first name when speaking to the little girl. Tina pointed to where Mrs. Das was purchasing something from one of the shirtless men who worked at the tea stall. Mr. Kapasi heard one of the shirtless men sing a phrase from a popular Hindi love song as Mrs. Das walked back to the car, but she did not appear to understand the words of the song, for she did not express irritation, or embarrassment, or react in any other way to the man's declarations.

He observed her. She wore a red-and-white-checkered skirt that stopped above her knees, slip-on shoes with a square wooden heel, and a close-fitting blouse styled like a man's undershirt. The blouse was decorated at chest-level with a calico appliqué in the shape of a strawberry. She was a short woman, with small hands like paws, her frosty pink fingernails painted to match her lips, and was slightly plump in her figure. Her hair, shorn only a little longer than her husband's, was parted far to one side. She was wearing large dark brown sunglasses with a pinkish tint to them, and carried a big straw bag, almost as big as her torso, shaped like a bowl, with a water bottle poking out of it. She walked slowly, carrying some puffed rice tossed with peanuts and chili peppers in a large packet made from newspapers. Mr. Kapasi turned to Mr. Das.

"Where in America do you live?"

"New Brunswick, New Jersey."

"Next to New York?"

"Exactly. I teach middle school there."

"What subject?"

GO ON TO THE NEXT PAGE

"Science. In fact, every year I take my students on a trip to the Museum of Natural History in New York City. In a way we have a lot in common, you could say, you and I. How long have you been a tour guide, Mr. Kapasi?"

"Five years."   105

Mrs. Das reached the car. "How long's the trip?" she asked, shutting the door.

"About two and a half hours," Mr. Kapasi replied.

At this Mrs. Das gave an impatient sigh, as if she had been traveling her whole life without pause. She fanned herself with a   110
folded Bombay film magazine written in English.

Question 3

American clergyman Harry Emerson Fosdick wrote, "I hate war for its consequences, for the lies it lives on and propagates, for the undying hatreds it arouses, for the dictatorships it puts in the place of democracies, and for the starvation that stalks after it." War, though, has proven a rich source of material for writers, perhaps because of those consequences.

Select a novel, play, or epic poem you have studied in which a war or its aftermath plays a significant role. Then, in a well-written essay, describe the role the war plays in the work and show how that role contributes to the meaning of the work as a whole. You may choose a work from the list below or another appropriate novel, play, or epic of similar literary quality. Avoid plot summary.

A Farewell to Arms	*Mrs. Dalloway*
A Separate Peace	*Nineteen Eighty-Four*
A Tale of Two Cities	*Obasan*
A Watch on the Rhine	*Paradise Lost*
All My Sons	*Pride and Prejudice*
All Quiet on the Western Front	*Regeneration*
Antigone	*Saint Joan*
Arms and the Man	*Slaughterhouse-Five*
Beloved	*The Aeneid*
Candide	*The English Patient*
Catch-22	*The Fall*
Cold Mountain	*The Ghost Road*
Doctor Zhivago	*The Iliad*
Don Quixote	*The Kite Runner*
Going After Cacciato	*The Naked and the Dead*
Henry V	*The Painted Bird*
Johnny Got His Gun	*The Red Badge of Courage*
Julius Caesar	*The Remains of the Day*
Lysistrata	*The Sun Also Rises*
Macbeth	*The Things They Carried*
Major Barbara	*The Tin Drum*
Mother Courage and Her Children	*War and Peace*

END OF EXAMINATION

ANSWERS AND EXPLANATIONS FOR SECTION I

MULTIPLE-CHOICE ANSWER KEY

Using the table below, determine how many questions you answered correctly, how many incorrectly. Then look over the answer explanations.

1. C	2. C	3. A	4. E	5. D
6. B	7. C	8. A	9. D	10. A
11. B	12. A	13. E	14. B	15. D
16. E	17. A	18. B	19. C	20. E
21. D	22. C	23. C	24. A	25. C
26. B	27. B	28. A	29. A	30. C
31. A	32. A	33. E	34. D	35. C
36. B	37. C	38. B	39. E	40. B
41. C	42. D	43. C	44. C	45. C
46. A	47. C	48. B	49. B	50. E
51. A	52. C	53. A	54. A	55. E

EXPLANATIONS FOR THE MULTIPLE-CHOICE ANSWERS

1. **ANSWER: C.** *A grammar question of a kind that nearly always appears on the test.* The referent in a question is almost never close to its pronoun. Here, what "all have given over" is "Love" (line 9) that is taking its "latest breath" and has a failing pulse. "Thou" is the person to whom the poem is addressed, and the other choices do not fit that test of being "given over."

2. **ANSWER: C.** *A structure/shift question.* The poem shifts between lines 8 and 9. At that point it shifts into a new sentence, takes on a new tone, moves from literal to metaphorical, and reverses the suggestion about what is to be done. Each part is made up of one sentence (although the semicolon in line 1 makes the first sentence more complex than the second) and ends with a period. Lines 1–8 are literal; lines 9–14 are figurative, building the allegory of dying Love. The speaker's apparent purpose in lines 1–8 is a goodbye, whether sincere or feigned. But the farewell of the first eight lines shifts in the last six to the suggestion that the love be brought back to life.

3. ANSWER: **A**. *A punctuation question to test the range of your reading.* Wide reading brings familiarity with conventions like this one. Words used allegorically are traditionally capitalized. None of the other choices include or imply any relation between the ideas in them and why a word would begin with a capital letter.

4. ANSWER: **E**. *A vocabulary question.* The phrase has a meaning closely related to "given up." That meaning can be deduced from the context, in which Passion, Faith, and Innocence are all behaving as though they have abandoned hope.

5. ANSWER: **D**. *A prosody question.* A reader would stress the line's opening word, "Now." But because the poem's rhythm is iambic, that word sits in an unstressed position. The opposite is true of the next word, "at." A strictly iambic reading of the line would neglect the key words "last" and "love" while accentuating the minor word "of." A "regular" reading of the line would force us into "Now AT the LAST gasp OF Love's LATEst BREATH"—far from the regular iambic pentameter of the lines in the other choices.

6. ANSWER: **B**. *A tone question.* To establish the speaker's tone, the poet uses (1) diction, choosing such words as "nay" and "yea," and the informal "jot"; (2) syntax, as in the repetition of "glad" to insist on his being untroubled, as though he is trying to convince himself; (3) rhythm, though the quickness of the lines, which results from the even rhythm. Although an argument could be made for the "tenderness" in C, we're looking for the best choice, and since there's no "confidence," B is better. In D, the cynicism might be possible, but "bewilderment" is not. In A and E, both words are inaccurate.

7. ANSWER: **C**. *A relationship question.* The reversal here is from the "there's no help" in line 1 to the possibility of recovery in line 14. B is opposite the actual relationship, E makes no sense since hopelessness cannot bring about a cure. A is wrong because the lines are not parallel. D is wrong because line 14 does include the metaphor of love and illness, but line 1 has none.

8. ANSWER: **A**. *A question about repetition/diction.* By repeating the word "now," the speaker insists on the need for immediate action to bring about the recovery. The other choices are contradicted by the poem.

9. ANSWER: **D**. *A vocabulary question: words with multiple meanings.* In this line, the word has the meaning of "still." The context eliminates the other choices.

10. ANSWER: **A**. *A question of tone and purpose.* The speaker here is suggesting, almost pleading, for his lover to keep the love alive. The words "stern," "grudging," and "didactic" eliminate B, C, and E, respectively, since those choices misstate the tone. An argument could be made for the "sharp" in D, but there is no admonition in the couplet, making A the best choice.

11. ANSWER: **B**. *A vocabulary question: words with multiple meanings.* The key is in the word "lies," which here means "lie" in the sense of "to lie

down." That eliminates A, C, and E. The word "stubbornly" eliminates D.

12. ANSWER: A. *An inference question.* The funeral in choice A is consistent with the words "consolation," "solemn," and especially "mourners." Nothing in the passage suggests a wedding or that the mother might be ill, and there is no mention of school. If the father and son were out for a day together, the father would be unlikely to send his son to play in the street.

13. ANSWER: E. *A question about metaphor and context.* The best choice is E, most likely echoing the boy's instructions from his mother before the story begins. Choice A has nothing to do with a brake, a tool to stop something. The boy has contact with neither the carriages nor the women in the pub, eliminating B and C. The reference to work in D comes in the boy's imagining about the future and not the immediate situation.

14. ANSWER: B. *An interpretation question.* Since the men are coming out of a pub, the obvious choice is B. The obvious choice isn't always the best choice, however, so we need to check the others. A and C are conceivable, but there's no reason for the men to be cautious with letters or with consoling touches. B is better because the men have to be cautious not to spill the beer. D won't work because there's no sign either that the journey is almost over or that the women react to any news. E is a common kind of distracter; it picks up a related word from another context—the "shawly women" inside the pub.

15. ANSWER: D. *A question about pattern.* The word "emphasize," taken with the word "repetition" in the question, makes D the best choice, and such details as the boy's pulling on his father's coat, as well as his apprehension about the trip home and his mother's reaction, reinforce the idea of discomfort.

16. ANSWER: E. *A characterization question.* The writer shows us a little through the father's limited dialogue but much more through the boy's narration of his father's actions at the counter and through what the boy implies about the father's actions in the past.

17. ANSWER: A. *A question of overall purpose and of tone.* The boy does nothing foolish here, and shows no dislike of his father, eliminating B and C. The passage presents no judgment of the boy's actions, so D is inaccurate. E won't work because we get reactions only from the boy. The details in the passage, though, from the women having drinks delivered to their carriage to the father's toying with his pint, lead up to the boy's drinking his father's beer.

18. ANSWER: B. *A question of interpretation and relationship.* Milton's line in B fits best because the "sweet" matches the father's enjoyment of the game of delaying drinking, and both "reluctant" and "amorous" fit with his actual purpose, which is to get great pleasure from drinking the pints. C can be eliminated because it is the father's first drink, not his third, as can D, because no one in the passage behaves in a vulgar way. While we might presume "affliction" and "distress" as the father's reaction to the death of a friend, other details, such as his playfulness

SCORING GUIDELINES FOR SECTION II

The score reported for each essay reflects the reader's judgment of the quality of the essay as a whole. Readers are instructed to reward the writers for what they do well. The score for an exceptionally well-written essay may be raised by one point. A poorly written essay can be scored no higher than a 3.

SCORING GUIDELINES FOR QUESTION 1

9–8 These essays compellingly treat both poems in some depth and are specific about how the two are different and how they are similar. They also discuss, explicitly, the relationship between the two and comment on the specific circumstances of the speakers. The scrutiny of the poems may or may not include technical comment on the form and prosody; if it does, the essay offers comment on the purpose or effectiveness of those aspects. Frequent references to the text are specific and fit the analytical context in which they appear. Although they may have flaws, these essays show a sensitive grasp of both poems and express it with dependable precision and maturity.

7–6 These essays present a rational and credible comparison and contrast between the two poems. Although in their interpretations they do not show the precision or the thoroughness of the top papers, they are thoughtful and attend to the tasks of the prompt. They enumerate and discuss both similarities and differences, although with less depth than the top essays. They may show less stylistic maturity or occasional wanderings. Nevertheless, they support their commentary clearly with specific and appropriate detail from the text, although possibly without the fine balance of the 8–9 papers. The writing style may be more workmanlike and have more hesitations but is still competent and generally comfortable.

5 These acceptable essays may be superficial in their understanding of explanations but they present plausible interpretations of both poems. They may slight the analysis of the relationship between the two poems or either the comparison or the contrast of the two. They may depend on generality instead of specificity in their comparisons and contrasts or marshal support that is too thin or only marginally appropriate to the student's commentary. They may fall into paraphrase, but that paraphrase, however overextended, will be in the attempted service of analysis. They may show a minor misreading of the poems. Although the writing may be unsophisticated and inexact or include distracting surface errors, it is still adequate to the expression of the writer's ideas.

4–3 These "lower-half" essays are incomplete in their understanding of either the prompt or the poems, or both. They may indulge in a more serious misreading of the poems or slight one of them completely. They often paraphrase more than they comment or comment without rooting their commentary in the text. The writing may fail to show organization and control over the content and the form. This is the highest score for an essay that discusses only one of the poems or whose organizational or mechanical weakness forces continuous backtracking and rereading.

2–1 These essays compound the weaknesses of the 3–4 papers. They may completely misconstrue the poems or pay little heed to the instructions. Typically they are unacceptable in form, in content, or both. While they address the prompt, they do so in a cursory, fleeting, or ineffective way. Essays scored 2 will include some analysis, however rudimentary. Essays scored 1 include no worthwhile comment on the poems.

0 These essays may refer to the prompt but make no attempt to respond to it.

— These essays are blank or do not mention the prompt or the poems.

SCORING GUIDELINES FOR QUESTION 2

9–8 These essays present a compelling discussion of how the author uses literary tools to establish character. They name the elements they choose, considering such devices as dialogue; direct description, including clothing; diction; tone; syntax; and the characters' interaction with each other or with the setting. These essays use brief, fitting, and specific details from the text, and they weave those references into their own commentary with skill. They offer, explicitly or implicitly, a persuasive case for their reading of the passage. They need not examine all the characters and need not examine equally those they do. The papers need not be free of error, but they show sophisticated—and in the case of an essay scored 9 admirable—command of language and of the conventions of composing literary analysis.

7–6 These essays offer a rational discussion of how the author uses literary tools to establish character, and they show a clear understanding of the passage and of some of the tools at work in it. They are accurate, although less specific and detailed than the 9–8 essays; they are capably written, although without the complexity and refinement of the top papers. These essays, clearly drafts, show less precision of expression, less complexity of writing style, but they present their ideas with enough support from the text to support and balance the writer's commentary on the passage. Essays scored 7 will reveal more development and more effective control of the language and structures of effective composition. Essays scored 6 are commonly less explicit in their examination and may rely more than necessarily on paraphrase, although still always in the service of analysis.

5 These essays propose a reading and response that are only adequate. They may be superficial or put forth supporting evidence from the text that is sufficient but little more. They may oversimplify the passage by focusing exclusively and less satisfactorily on only one character or slight the piece's complexity by overemphasis on one device. They offer analysis but root it less securely in specifics from the passage, and they may fall in places into overparaphrasing. The control of the tools of effective communication is adequate, but the writing may show need of more revision—both deep and surface—than essays scored higher.

4–3 These essays offer an inadequate understanding of the prompt, of the passage, or both. They may misconstrue the writer's presentation of the characters or be unable to tie that presentation to the tools she uses to accomplish it. The misreading may be significant or the essay may lapse into paraphrase for its own sake. Some may find details that, in reality, don't exist in the passage, or attempt to take the story beyond what appears in the passage. These papers may suffer from unnecessary repetition or disorder or show consistent errors that impede reading.

2–1 These essays may be unacceptably brief or have an accumulation of errors that prevents understanding. They may show a complete misreading of the passage or fail to include details from it. Especially in the case of essays scored 2, an attempt at analysis appears, but the attempt does not succeed. Essays scored 1 show a particular incoherence.

0 Although these essays may refer to the prompt, they do not address it.

— These essays are either left blank or are completely off-topic.

SCORING GUIDELINES FOR QUESTION 3

9–8 These persuasive essays identify a war, battle, or other military action in an appropriate novel, play, or epic. They explain with precision and rich concrete detail from the text the role the war plays in it. They articulate clearly a meaning of the work as a whole and show compellingly how the role they have defined of the war relates to it. While it's possible the war itself is not central to the literary work, it is to these essays. They are not without flaw, but they are focused and organized, and alternate with skill between the details of the text and the writer's comment on that detail. They show that the writer reads with perception and has a practiced and sophisticated control over the techniques of expressing that perception. A paper scored 9 will show particular polish and grace.

7–6 These essays present a rational and credible explanation of the war's impact on a clearly stated meaning of the work. The account of that relationship may be more mechanical or less smoothly articulated, and the essays less thorough or specific than the top papers, but they demonstrate both an accurate reading of the work and sufficient control over the elements of writing about literature. Essays scored 7 will have stronger textual support for their claims and, generally, more expertise of expression than those scored 6.

5 These acceptable essays may be superficial in their expression of the relationship of the war to a meaning of the work. They may overexplain the obvious or belabor predictable ideas rather than offer insight. Plot summary may play too large a role, but plot summary is still linked to an attempt at analysis. While the writing may be inexact in diction and lack grace in syntax, it is still adequate to the expression of the writer's ideas.

4–3 These "lower-half" essays are incomplete, either in their understanding of the prompt or of the works they purport to analyze, or both. They may choose a conflict they cannot successfully relate to a meaning of the work or they may be unable to articulate such a meaning clearly. Often they will relate a battle or campaign at great, unnecessary length and fail to comment meaningfully on its role in the work. They may fail to go beyond restating what is evident in a plot line or be carried away by plot summary. The writing may fail to show organization and control over the content and the form. This is the highest score for an essay that avoids identifying a meaning of the work as a whole or whose organizational or mechanical weakness forces continuous rereading and backtracking.

2–1 These essays compound the weaknesses of the 4–3 papers. They may completely misconstrue the actual purpose of an author's using the events of a war or pay little heed to the instructions. Typically they are unacceptable in form, in content, or both. While they address to the prompt, they do so in a cursory, fleeting, or ineffective way. Essays scored 2 will include some analysis, however rudimentary. Essays scored 1 offer no worthwhile comment on the poems.

0 These essays may refer to the prompt but make no attempt to respond to it.

— These essays are blank or do not mention the prompt or the poems.

CALCULATING YOUR AP EXAM GRADE ON THE DIAGNOSTIC TEST

Please keep in mind that these numbers are approximate. Two variables affect the computation every year: the number of multiple-choice questions and the difficulty levels of the essays. There is a slight curve created every year in terms of the numbers. However, remember that earning 15 points on the three essays combined and getting 55 percent right and marking as many as 11 wrong answers on the multiple-choice questions will generally produce a grade of 3.

SCORING THE MULTIPLE-CHOICE SECTION

$$\underline{\hspace{3cm}} - (1/4 \times \underline{\hspace{3cm}}) = \underline{\hspace{3cm}}$$

number correct   number incorrect   multiple-choice score

SCORING THE FREE-RESPONSE SECTION

$$\underline{\hspace{2cm}} + \underline{\hspace{2cm}} + \underline{\hspace{2cm}} = \underline{\hspace{2cm}}$$

Question 1   Question 2   Question 3   total essay score
(0–9 score)   (0–9 score)   (0–9 score)

CALCULATING THE COMPOSITE SCORE

$$1.23 \times \frac{}{\text{multiple-choice score}} = \underline{\hspace{3cm}}$$

weighted section I score

$$3.05 \times \frac{}{\text{free-response score}} = \underline{\hspace{3cm}}$$

weighted section II score

$$\underline{\hspace{3cm}} + \underline{\hspace{3cm}} = \underline{\hspace{3cm}}$$

weighted section I   weighted section II   composite score

DETERMINING YOUR AP EXAM GRADE

You now have a number between 0 and 150. The composite scores are divided into five ranges, one for each AP grade. Each year that scale is adjusted. Generally, it goes like this:

Composite Score Range	AP Grade
112–150	5
95–111	4
76–94	3
50–75	2
0–49	1

Part II

Reviewing for the AP English Literature and Composition Exam

THINGS YOU SHOULD KNOW

Knowing how to identify literary devices in a text is only one part of conducting analysis. The overall purpose of analysis is to understand how an author develops meaning and suggests tone through diction and literary techniques. Many students worry that they won't have enough time to memorize the definitions of every literary term before the test, or they fear they won't be able to identify the devices in a passage. Don't panic! The purpose of the exam is not to stump you with a never-ending litany of questions about terminology. Besides, what would be the purpose of being able to identify a simile if you couldn't explain why it was being used? Literary terms make the job of analysis easier by providing a common vocabulary for discussing literature. That vocabulary is a tool for analysis, not the purpose of analysis. Included in this chapter is a list of the literary terms you will need for analyzing prose and poetry selections. But first you should review tone, which is key to literary analysis.

TONE

Tone can be a difficult literary concept to grasp, but understanding what tone is—and is not—goes a long way toward understanding what the author is saying. Many students confuse tone with mood. Although different, both tone and mood can have the same emotional impact. The author's *attitude,* stated or implied, toward a subject is referred to as tone. Some possible attitudes are optimism, earnestness, bitterness, humor, and exuberance. An author's tone can be revealed through choice of words and details. If the subject is an abstract concept such as death, discerning the tone of such a passage requires figuring out the narrator's or speaker's attitude or feelings about death. (The word "narrator" generally refers to the person telling a story, while the word "speaker" refers to the person from whose perspective a poem is told. Keep in mind that the narrator or speaker is not always the same as the author.) Does the narrator seem afraid of death? Does the narrator see death as a natural part of life? To find out, you must look for clues to how the narrator feels about death. Is the narrator reliable? Look at the opening lines from Edgar Allan Poe's "The Tell-Tale Heart":

> True!—nervous—very, very dreadfully nervous I had been and am; but why *will* you say that I am mad? The disease had sharpened my senses—not destroyed—not dulled them. Above all was the sense of hearing acute. I heard all things in the heaven and in the earth. I heard many things in hell. How, then, am I mad? Hearken!

and observe how healthily—how calmly I can tell you the whole story.

From the beginning the reader understands that the narrator is mentally ill. The dashes to represent fragmented ideas and the description of the exaggeration of the senses are details that the author includes to let the reader know that, despite the narrator's claims, he is indeed insane. Determining whether the narrator is reliable is not usually this easy. Still, when you begin reading a passage, you should always separate the narrator's thoughts from the author's thoughts. In essence, you are deconstructing the passage, looking at its parts in order to determine its overall meaning.

Tone is created through words. All words have a denotative meaning—that is, every word has a literal definition. Many words also have a connotative meaning—that is, a word, along with its literal, denotative meaning, can have a positive or negative feeling associated with it. For example, the word "lady" has a denotative meaning much the same as the word "woman." Both are defined as a female person. However, does one word sound more positive? Let's add another word that means female to the group, the word "broad," a slang term used as a slur. The connotation, or feeling, is negative. If an author uses the word "lady" in reference to a character, the attitude toward the character is much more positive than would be the attitude toward a character referred to as a "broad." Pay particular attention to the connotative powers of words. In general, if the author feels strongly about a particular subject, he or she will want you to feel the same way toward that subject.

Edgar Allan Poe is often a favorite of those who like a good horror story. Many of Poe's stories center around the subject of death, and the tone he creates is one of apprehension and melancholy. Continuing with "The Tell-Tale Heart":

> It is impossible to say how first the idea entered my brain; but once conceived, it haunted me day and night. Object there was none. Passion there was none. I loved the old man. He had never wronged me. He had never given me insult. For his gold I had no desire. I think it was his eye! yes, it was this! One of his eyes resembled that of a vulture—a pale eye, with a film over it. Whenever it fell upon me, my blood ran cold; and so by degrees—very gradually—I made up my mind to take the life of the old man, and thus rid myself of the eye forever.

As the story proceeds, it becomes clear that it is not enough to kill the old man because of his deformity, or "evil eye," as the narrator describes it. Instead, the old man must be hacked into pieces and hidden under the floorboards of his own home! We know through the narrator's actions that he is indeed insane, though he professes that he is not. The narrator views his actions as inevitable and tries to justify the old man's brutal murder. Is this the attitude toward death that we get from the author? No. This is the attitude of the narrator. But what is the author's attitude?

No doubt I now grew *very* pale; —but I talked more fluently, and with a heightened voice. Yet the sound increased—and what could I do? It was a *low, dull, quick sound—much such a sound as a watch makes when enveloped in cotton.* I gasped for breath—and yet the officers heard it not. I talked more quickly—more vehemently; but the noise steadily increased. I arose and argued about trifles, in a high key and with violent gesticulations; but the noise steadily increased. Why *would* they not be gone? I paced the floor to and fro with heavy strides, as if excited to fury by the observations of the men—but the noise steadily increased. Oh God! what *could* I do? I foamed—I raved—I swore!

We know from the actions of the narrator that the author wants us to understand that the motives for the murder are not justified and that murder is an insane act. Death is not something that is deserved or that always comes upon us naturally or peacefully. The tone of the story is then disturbing and melancholic.

Because the reader and the author often have the same feelings about a character or a situation, tone and mood often become confused. Mood refers to the climate of feeling or atmosphere in a literary work. It is the overall sense a reader gets when reading a particular passage or poem. The choices of setting, objects, details, images, and words all help to create a specific mood. Keep in mind that how you, the reader, feel about a subject is not necessarily the same as how the author feels about it, but the two may coincide. When we read horror stories, we are often filled with dread. We may even feel suspense and fear. That's what the author wants you to feel. And that's why mood and tone are often described with the same words.

Determining the tone of a literary work can be difficult. This is especially true of poetry. A T-chart can be very helpful in understanding tone. Draw a *T* on a piece of paper and label the left side *positive,* the right side *negative.* As you read, list words with a positive or a negative connotation (emotion) on the appropriate side of your T-chart. Before long, you will begin to see that one side of your T-Chart has grown a lot longer than the other. You can then begin to find the right tone words. When you write about tone, refer to your T-chart for specific words to support your conclusions.

Some writing doesn't have a positive or negative tone; the tone is said to be neutral. You commonly encounter this type of writing in learning materials such as handbooks, textbooks, and manuals. They can be described as didactic or dry.

In some works of literature there is often a shift in tone. This is especially common in poetry. A poem may begin, say, rather sadly, then shift to a scene or statement of hope. There can also be more than one shift in tone. When we discuss poetry in more depth, we will take up the importance of identifying shifts in poetry.

Below is a list of tone words divided into three general categories: positive, negative, and neutral. Be sure you know the meanings of these tone words. You need a sophisticated vocabulary for literary analysis. Simply saying the tone is positive or negative or neutral doesn't provide any clarity. In addition, nuanced vocabulary to describe tone will give your writing a boost. The multiple-choice section of the AP exam will include many questions testing your ability to discern tone and understand words in context—there is one question of this type for nearly every passage.

TONE VOCABULARY

POSITIVE ATTITUDE WORDS

amused	exuberant	loving	sentimental
boisterous	exultant	merry	sympathetic
cheery	fanciful	mirthful	tickled
compassionate	festive	nostalgic	whimsical
complimentary	flattering	optimistic	wistful
confident	genial	passionate	witty
effusive	hopeful	playful	
elated	jocular	proud	
enthusiastic	lighthearted	sanguine	

NEGATIVE ATTITUDE WORDS

accusing	condescending	exacerbated	incensed
admonitory	contemptuous	exasperated	indignant
anxious	critical	facetious	inflammatory
apprehensive	cynical	fearful	insolent
arrogant	depressed	flippant	irate
ashamed	derisive	foreboding	irreverent
bantering	despairing	furious	irritated
bitter	disconcerted	gloomy	livid
chagrined	disdainful	hopeless	manipulative
concerned	disgusted	humorless	melancholic
condemnatory	disturbed	incendiary	mock-serious

lines) with the rhyme scheme *abbaabba*. The octave generally includes the "problem" that the sonnet will develop. It is followed by a sestet (six lines), which has as its rhyme scheme *cdcdcd* (or some variation thereof). The "problem" is resolved in the sestet.

STANZA: A group of lines that forms one division of a poem.

SYMBOL: An object that signifies something greater than itself. For example, the bald eagle is often used as a symbol of the United States.

SYNECDOCHE: A figure of speech in which a part is used for the whole—for example, "All hands on deck." (We assume the sailors' bodies will follow.)

THEME: An insight into life conveyed by a poem or story. The theme is the main point the author wants to make with the reader, and is often a basic truth, an acknowledgment of our humanity, or a reminder of human beings' shortcomings. This general insight is usually about life, society, or human nature. Themes often explore timeless and universal ideas. Most themes are implied rather than stated explicitly. Short works of fiction may have only one or two themes; however, a novel may include many themes because of the number and depth of the characters and the numerous events within the plot.

VERSE: Lines of poetry or metrical language in general, in contrast to prose.

A Closer Look at Multiple-Choice Questions

You are allotted sixty minutes for Section I of the AP exam, which consists of approximately fifty-five multiple-choice questions based on four or five selections. The selections are drawn from poetry, prose, and drama by American and British writers from the sixteenth century to the present. You are not allowed to bring a dictionary or thesaurus, so it is in your best interest to be familiar with how language has been used over that span of time. A good anthology, such as *Perrine's Literature: Structure, Sound, and Sense* by Thomas R. Arp and Greg Johnson, is invaluable. There you will find gathered in one place literature that represents a variety of genres, time periods, writers, and styles.

The multiple-choice questions are designed to test your ability to read analytically, to recognize literary devices and their role in the work in question, and to understand the techniques writers use to express their ideas. For success with the multiple-choice questions, practice close reading under timed conditions. Answering fifty-five questions in sixty minutes gives you little time to think about each question.

Your score on this section of the exam will be 45 percent of your total score.

The Importance of Annotation

Make it a habit to annotate while you read. Annotation—highlighting, circling, or underlining words or phrases and writing your thoughts in the margins—is key to developing close reading skills. I begin each school year with several weeks of highlighting diction (to find the tone), circling or underlining metaphors and similes (imagery), and making brief notes in the margins (connecting with the text for meaning). These marks and scribbled notes are annotations.

Have you ever found yourself reading and suddenly a character or event reminds you of an experience you have had? Have you ever read a line of poetry and said, "Huh?" These are perfect places to annotate. If a word in the text sounds like gibberish, underline it and place a question mark in the margin. As you read on, you may be able to understand the line. If not, the question mark is a reminder to bring the word up during a class discussion. Either way, you are learning to pay *close attention* to what you are reading. When you come across a line of prose that is particularly descriptive or comical or that prompts you to say, "Aha!" make a brief note—"vivid colors," "slapstick action," "he confesses his love"—in the margin.

When you annotate, you are interacting with what you are reading. You begin to pay more attention to diction, imagery, similes and metaphors, and a host of other literary devices. When you slow down just long enough to highlight or jot down a note or a question in the margin, you will notice more and more details. Connecting to the text helps you remember details and recognize ideas within the text.

There is such a thing as too much annotation. When you are learning to annotate, it often happens that you look back over a passage you have read and see nothing but an ocean of highlighter fluid and a zillion scribbled notes. Don't worry! Eventually you'll learn to recognize what is and is not important.

An Example of Annotation

The following is a passage from "The Story of an Hour" by Kate Chopin. Pencil in hand, annotate it as you read. When you are finished, look at the sample annotated version of the passage. No peeking! The idea is to compare your annotations with ours.

Knowing that Mrs. Mallard was afflicted with a heart trouble, great care was taken to break to her as gently as possible the news of her husband's death.

It was her sister Josephine who told her, in broken sentences, veiled hints that revealed in half concealing. Her husband's friend   5
Richards was there, too, near her. It was he who had been in the newspaper office when intelligence of the railroad disaster was received, with Brently Mallard's name leading the list of "killed." He had only taken the time to assure himself of its truth by a second telegram, and had hastened to forestall any less careful,   10
less tender friend in bearing the sad message.

She did not hear the story as many women have heard the same, with a paralyzed inability to accept its significance. She wept at once, with sudden, wild abandonment, in her sister's arms. When the storm of grief had spent itself she went away to   15
her room alone. She would have no one follow her.

There stood, facing the open window, a comfortable, roomy armchair. Into this she sank, pressed down by a physical exhaustion that haunted her body and seemed to reach into her soul.   20

She could see in the open square before her house the tops of trees that were all aquiver with the new spring life. The delicious breath of rain was in the air. In the street below a peddler was crying his wares. The notes of a distant song which some one was singing reached her faintly, and countless sparrows were   25
twittering in the eaves.

There were patches of blue sky showing here and there through the clouds that had met and piled one above the other in the west facing her window.

She sat with her head thrown back upon the cushion of the   30
chair, quite motionless, except when a sob came up into her

throat and shook her, as a child who has cried itself to sleep continues to sob in its dreams.

She was young, with a fair, calm face, whose lines bespoke repression and even a certain strength. But now there was a dull stare in her eyes, whose gaze was fixed away off yonder on one of those patches of blue sky. It was not a glance of reflection, but rather indicated a suspension of intelligent thought.

There was something coming to her and she was waiting for it, fearfully. What was it? She did not know; it was too subtle and elusive to name. But she felt it, creeping out of the sky, reaching toward her through the sounds, the scents, the color that filled the air.

Now her bosom rose and fell tumultuously. She was beginning to recognize this thing that was approaching to possess her, and she was striving to beat it back with her will—as powerless as her two white slender hands would have been.

When she abandoned herself a little whispered word escaped her slightly parted lips. She said it over and over under her breath: "Free, free, free!" The vacant stare and the look of terror that had followed it went from her eyes. They stayed keen and bright. Her pulses beat fast, and the coursing blood warmed and relaxed every inch of her body.

She did not stop to ask if it were not a monstrous joy that held her. A clear and exalted perception enabled her to dismiss the suggestion as trivial.

She knew that she would weep again when she saw the kind, tender hands folded in death; the face that had never looked save with love upon her, fixed and gray and dead. But she saw beyond that bitter moment a long procession of years to come that would belong to her absolutely. And she opened and spread her arms out to them in welcome.

Now that you have read the passage and annotated your connections to it, let's look at a sample of what an annotated version of the passage might look like.

weak

Knowing that Mrs. Mallard was afflicted with a heart trouble, great care was taken to break to her as gently as possible the news of her husband's death.

It was her sister Josephine who told her, in broken sentences, veiled hints that revealed in half concealing. Her husband's friend   5
Richards was there, too, near her. It was he who had been in the newspaper office when intelligence of the railroad disaster was received, with Brently Mallard's name leading the list of "killed."
He had only taken the time to assure himself of its truth by a
in the past? second telegram, and had hastened to forestall any less careful,   10
less tender friend in bearing the sad message.   *husband dead*

She did not hear the story as many women have heard the same, with a paralyzed inability to accept its significance. She wept at once, with sudden, wild abandonment, in her sister's arms. When the storm of grief had spent itself she went away to   15
her room alone. She would have no one follow her.   *not like other women?*

There stood, facing the open window, a comfortable, roomy armchair. Into this she sank, pressed down by a physical exhaustion that haunted her body and seemed to reach into her soul.   *Personification*   20

She could see in the open square before her house the tops of trees that were all aquiver with the new spring life. The delicious breath of rain was in the air. In the street below a peddler was
? crying his wares. The notes of a distant song which some one was singing reached her faintly, and countless sparrows were   25
twittering in the eaves.   *Spring life v. Death of husband*

There were patches of blue sky showing here and there
personified through the clouds that had met and piled one above the other in the west facing her window.

She sat with her head thrown back upon the cushion of the   30
chair, quite motionless, except when a sob came up into her throat and shook her, as a child who has cried itself to sleep continues to sob in its dreams.   *simile*   — *so, not weak?*
Young/spring ——— She was young, with a fair, calm face, whose lines bespoke
?? — repression and even a certain strength. But now there was a dull   35
stare in her eyes, whose gaze was fixed away off yonder on one of   *diction (south or west)*
those patches of blue sky. It was not a glance of reflection, but rather indicated a suspension of intelligent thought. *more nature*

There was something coming to her and she was waiting for it, fearfully. What was it? She did not know; it was too subtle and   40
elusive to name. But she felt it, creeping out of the sky, reaching toward her through the sounds, the scents, the color that filled   *suspense!*
the air.

Now her bosom rose and fell tumultuously. She was beginning to recognize this thing that was approaching to   45
possess her, and she was striving to beat it back with her will—as   *Diction—Is she in danger?*
powerless as her two white slender hands would have been.

When she abandoned herself a little whispered word escaped her slightly parted lips. She said it over and over under her breath: "Free, free, free!" The vacant stare and the look of terror   50
that had followed it went from her eyes. They stayed keen and bright. Her pulses beat fast, and the coursing blood warmed and   *free v. repression*
relaxed every inch of her body.

E also points toward a contrast in meanings; however, antithesis is the juxtaposition of opposing ideas in balanced phrases or clauses.

3. Lines 12-16 ("She did not hear . . . have no one follow her") suggest that Mrs. Mallard
   (A) is stronger than others believe her to be
   (B) is mentally unstable
   (C) reacted to the news of her husband's death as any woman would
   (D) feels hopelessly lost without her husband
   (E) is in shock over the death of her husband

ANSWER: A. The statement that she "would have no one follow her" seems rather commanding in tone and suggests that Mrs. Mallard is not as fragile as previously supposed. There is no mention or suggestion of mental instability (B). Answer C is incorrect because the passage notes that Mrs. Mallard doesn't react as another women might to the death of her husband. Answer D is simply not supported by the passage. Answer E says that Mrs. Mallard is in shock, but she doesn't show physical signs of shock, and wanting to be alone doesn't indicate that she is in shock.

4. In line 24, the word "crying" means
   (A) lamenting
   (B) weeping
   (C) shouting
   (D) howling
   (E) singing

ANSWER: C. This is a question that requires you to consider other definitions of a commonly used word. Answers A and B are too similar in meaning to "crying" and suggests the peddler is sad, but the passage doesn't give the reader information about the peddler's emotional state. Answer E is an action one would take if he or she was happy, but again we know nothing about the peddler's emotional state. Answer D is a loud sound similar to a shout; however, the word is associated with pain or distress. The only word in the list that suggests a loud sound but is the least emotional is the word "shout," answer C.

5. When saying, "whose lines bespoke repression" (lines 34–35), the narrator does which of the following?
   (A) makes a general reference to the overall condition of women
   (B) introduces the idea of slavery
   (C) emphasizes the theme of death
   (D) suggests the need for change
   (E) connects a youthful appearance with nature

ANSWER: A. Line 35 begins to hint at the overall theme of the story. As readers we are, at first, perhaps shocked by the word "repression." The word has a negative connotation, and the line suggests that Mrs. Mallard has been controlled or dominated by something or someone. In this case, as the passage continues, it is clear that her husband and the institution of marriage have controlled her. There are little hints within the story that point toward an earlier time in history when the use of the telegraph and the railroad were common. Answer E has nothing to do with repression, but rather, with a new beginning. Answer D is too vague in meaning. The phrase doesn't emphasize death (C), which is a different state than repression. Answer B would be the best distractor because slavery is, in fact, a state of repression. But the best answer is A because the repression seems to center on a restraint that is not physical but social, one common during a period when women had few rights during marriage. Mrs. Mallard is "free" only after the death of her husband.

6. The news of Mr. Mallard's death is in contrast to the narrator's description of
   (A) a storm
   (B) Mrs. Mallard's emotional state
   (C) Mrs. Mallard's sister
   (D) Mrs. Mallard's physical health
   (E) nature

ANSWER: E. Lines 1–20 focus on the news of Mr. Mallard's death and Mrs. Mallard's emotional response to the news. Lines 21–29 repeatedly mention nature with its "delicious breath," "new spring life," "distant song," and "patches of blue sky." All are in direct contrast to the idea of death. Answer A suggests there is a storm; however, the only storm is that of grief (line 15). Answer B suggests that Mrs. Mallard's emotional state at hearing the news of her husband's death would be the opposite of grief, which is not the case in the beginning of the passage. There is not enough information on Mrs. Mallard's sister (C), and answer D suggests that Mrs. Mallard's physical health is deteriorating, which it is not.

7. In lines 59–62, the narrator conveys a sense of
   (A) sanguinity
   (B) nostalgia
   (C) contentment
   (D) skepticism
   (E) arrogance

ANSWER: A. Mrs. Mallard's emotional state at the end of the passage suggests that she is welcoming what lies ahead of her now that her husband is dead. She doesn't look back to the past with longing, as answer B would suggest. She is not skeptical (answer D) about what awaits her. There is no doubt that she feels she is in control of her own life now, but Mrs. Mallard doesn't show any sense of arrogance, as answer E would suggest. Answer C is a good distractor in that she indeed seems content, but she is in a heightened emotional state that goes beyond contentment. The word "sanguinity" means cheerfully optimistic, and Mrs. Mallard is indeed optimistic about her future.

8. All of the following are personified in the passage EXCEPT
   (A) "rain" (line 23)
   (B) "hands" (line 58)
   (C) freedom (lines 41–42)
   (D) "heart-trouble" (line 1)
   (E) "physical exhaustion" (lines 18–19)

ANSWER: **D.** The only answer can be heart trouble. "The delicious breath of rain" (A), "the kind, tender hands folded in death" (B), freedom "creeping out of the sky, reaching toward her through the sounds, the scents, the color that filled the air" (C), and "a physical exhaustion that haunted her body and seemed to reach into her soul" (E) are examples of personification.

9. What does the pronoun "it" in lines 39–41 refer to?
   (A) freedom
   (B) death
   (C) hope
   (D) misfortune
   (E) fear

ANSWER: **A.** Chopin here offers an unusual description of the feeling of freedom. It is intentional because the narrator wants the reader to understand that "being free" as a woman is both liberating and frightening. In a close reading of the text, one would notice the use of the telegraph to receive information about Mr. Mallard's death. Even if one didn't notice this detail, the lines after 39–43 make clear that the emotion Mrs. Mallard was fearful of was being "free." During the late 1800s and early 1900s, women were expected to marry; all property that belonged to a woman before marriage became the property of her husband. A married woman had legal power only when she became a widow. It was indeed a "monstrous joy" because Mrs. Mallard's new sense of freedom was a direct consequence of her husband's death.

THE POETRY ESSAY QUESTION

Your preparation for Section II of the AP exam should include a heavy emphasis on honing your writing skills. Over the course of the school year, you will have many opportunities to write about literary works. The type of writing you do depends on its purpose, but may include one of the following:

- **WRITING TO UNDERSTAND:** writing that responds to literature through reading journals, annotative reading, and free writing
- **WRITING TO EXPLAIN:** essays that focus on a particular aspect of language or structure in literature and on the analysis of a written passage
- **WRITING TO EVALUATE:** essays that demonstrate an ability to develop and explain a position and to assess the connections between literature and social and cultural values

As you practice your ability to understand, explain, and evaluate both poetry and prose passages, remember that the work of analysis is only part of the scoring criteria. The scoring also takes into account the clarity of your writing and your stylistic maturity. AP readers look for the following:

- Do you balance the general with the specific in your analysis—do you use general statements and then provide specific examples to support those statements?
- Do you use transitions effectively so the reader understands the logical connections between general statements and specific details and among related ideas?
- Is your vocabulary strong? Do you use words that are vague such as "things," "like," "good," and "bad"? Is your vocabulary rich and varied? If you wait to apply new words until the time of the AP exam, you will likely feel uncomfortable using them and run the risk of sounding unsure of the meaning or of trying to impress your reader. Build them into your vocabulary now. When you encounter a new word, try to use it in your next writing assignment or class discussion. The more familiar you are with new words, the more likely you will be to use them in your writing on the test.
- Do you use a variety of sentence structures in your writing? Don't be afraid to use, say, an appositive or an infinitive or a variety of short and long sentences. Your writing will be more interesting and demonstrate your control of language.
- Does your paper sound like *you*? In essence, this asks if your writing has voice. If you have developed a sense of voice, it will show in your choice of vocabulary, sentence arrangement, and organization. When someone can recognize your writing without

seeing your name on the paper, you are well on your way to developing both a voice and stylistic maturity.

GETTING A HANDLE ON A POEM

The first essay question is based on poetry. Poetry can be difficult to understand, especially if it uses unfamiliar vocabulary or allusions. It's always a good idea to have a dictionary handy when reading poetry, though you won't have that luxury when taking the AP exam.

Thomas Arp and Greg Johnson, the authors of *Perrine's Literature: Structure, Sound, and Sense* suggest that "poetry might be defined as a kind of language that says *more* and says it *more intensely* than does ordinary language." Indeed, poets choose their words very, very carefully in order to convey a specific meaning and evoke specific emotions. As a consequence, poetry needs to be read slowly and thoughtfully. Although poems often contain far fewer words than the average short story, they can convey greater emotion and reflect more profound themes.

To get the most out of a poem, try following these steps as you read:

- Read the title of the poem and consider its possible meaning.
- Read the poem through once, and then paraphrase it in your own words. What is the poem saying?
- Note the diction. Is the connotation of the words generally positive or negative?
- Look—and listen—for poetic devices such as rhyme, similes, metaphors, personification, symbolism, allusions, alliteration, assonance, and onomatopoeia.
- Determine who is speaking to determine the point of view. Is it a child, an invalid, a grandmother, a dog?
- Determine the subject—for example, love, death, a town, a time of day—of the poem.
- Use your tone vocabulary to determine the speaker's attitude toward the subject.
- Locate shifts—for example, changes in time, place, speaker, tone— in the poem.
- Return to the title. Has the meaning or significance of the title changed since the first time you read it?
- Put it all together—what is the poet saying about his subject, the theme of the poem?

All of these aspects of a poem are essential to determining its overall meaning. Although it is important to identify poetic devices such as similes, personification, and onomatopoeia, *your essay should not be a laundry list of devices*. It's more important that you understand how a particular device contributes to the overall meaning of the poem. If the poem includes alliteration, why did the poet use it? If there is imagery in the poem, what connotation does the imagery have? How does the imagery add to the reader's experience of the poem? Analysis is not simply identifying various literary and poetic devices; it is determining how those devices add to the overall meaning of the prose or poem.

succumbed to the poisonous gas. As the speaker explains, "In all my dreams, before my helpless sight, / He plunges at me, guttering, choking, drowning." He invites the reader to join him in his nightmare and see the dead with agony etched in their faces. The tone is one of revulsion toward the act of war. The overall structure of the poem begins with a rather unexpected image of soldiers exhausted and "bent double" like old men with uniforms hanging on their emaciated bodies like "sacks." The image of these soldiers is not the image we expect, which echoes the point the poem makes—war is never what we "expect." A shift to present tense signals the reader that a decisive moment for the soldiers is occurring—live with a mask or die from gas. There is no glorious confrontation with the enemy in human form, just a poisonous gas. The speaker then shifts to his nightmares of dying soldiers and ends with a plea to the reader to tell war as it is—abominable. The use of the words "devil" and "sick of sin" suggests that war is a sin and that to encourage the idea that to die in war is glorious is a sin as well.

In Simic's poem a ten-year-old boy with a great imagination and the idea that war is an adventurous act becomes an "old soldier" as he fights many imaginary battles and kills thousands in his garden at home. His mother pulls him away from his games of war into the reality of war itself as the air raid begins, but all that the speaker seems to notice is the flowering cherry trees, the sky full of birds and the ants at their feet still "their usual serene selves." He seems oblivious to the real consequences of war. War is child's play to the young, and the disillusionment so apparent in Owen's poem is obviously missing in Simic's. The boy continues in his make-believe world when he confesses to the reader that his sword is made of cardboard but that its handle was "painted gold," echoing the sentiment that all is not what it seems. He mentions the fact that he is in need of a horse to continue in his imaginative play and morbidly suggests a horse he has seen pulling the hearse "with a merry wave of his tail." The boy does not see the painful reality of death that accompanies war. The tone is nonchalant and is in direct contrast to "Dulce et Decorum Est." The speaker in "Old Soldier" is playing out a scene that the real soldier in "Dulce et Decorum Est" warns about. "Old Soldier" seems to suggest that the acts of war will continue because some children (like the speaker) never learn the hard realities of war or are allowed to indulge in imaginative play that promulgates the idea that war is glorious and death an illusion. The boy dismisses the "crumbling walls," "flying cinders," and "hearse"—the realities of war—and instead focuses on the "quick errands" of ants, the sky full of birds, and the "merry wave" of the horse's tail that pulls the hearse.

COMMENT

This essay effectively compares and contrasts both poems. The writer understands that the subject of both poems is war, but that they are told from different points of view and, therefore, create different tones (repugnance in one, nonchalance in the other). The essay gives many examples from both poems of imagery and the effect it has in creating tone. The essay effectively analyzes how point of view, diction, and imagery affect the overall themes of the poems, and it demonstrates the maturity of the writer's style.

A STUDENT ESSAY SCORED 6

"Dulce et Decorum Est" by Wilfred Owen and "Old Soldier" by Charles Simic have many similarities and differences. Both poems are about war, but one poem tells about war in a very vivid way and the other is told by a young boy who likes to play at war but isn't actually a soldier in a war. The two poems are written from two different point of views which has an effect on the tone in both poems as well.

Wilfred Owen explores the violence of war through the point of view of a soldier who is facing the realities of war, in particular deadly gas that can drown you "under a green sea" (line 14). The soldier describes the terrible condition he and his fellow soldiers are in. "Men marched asleep" (line 5) are further described as "Bent double, like old beggars under sacks" (line 1). The soldier describes the horror of seeing one of the soldiers die from gas and the reader can't help but grimace in horror. He makes war sound so terrible that to think about war as being something glorious doesn't seem right. The soldier even says that if you had really experienced war as he had, you wouldn't tell children "the old Lie" (line 27) that "Dulce et decorum est / Pro patria mori"—"It is sweet and becoming to die for one's country." The tone is depressing and horrific.

In Charles Simic's poem "Old Soldier" war is seen through the eyes of a ten-year-old boy. He is a boy during a war; however, he is the old soldier mentioned in the title because he says that by the time he was ten, he had "fought in hundreds of battles, / Had innumerable wounds, / Had slain thousands." Of course, he was only ten and these were imaginary battles. To the boy war is seen as exciting. He does not seem to understand or even notice the realities of war. He is not scared during the air raids and he does not seem to understand the significance of a hearse going down the street. He is a part of an imaginary world, the world that Wilfred Owen's soldier warns the reader about.

There is not a lot of vivid imagery in "Old Soldier"; however, the speaker mentions that the cherry trees are blossoming (line 7) and the ants are continuing their errands as if nothing has happened (line 15). He seems to notice only the positive aspects of the world around him and not the reality of war with its crumbling walls and hearses. Although both poems are about war, they are viewed in opposite ways. Owen wants to warn the reader about the true horror of war and Simic seems to want to focus on the innocence of war.

COMMENT

This essay does compare and contrast the two poems and understands the general differences between the two poems based on the different points of view. There is some analysis within the essay—"He is a part of an imaginary world, the world that Wilfred Owen's soldier warns the reader about." The style is not as mature as an essay that receives a higher score, but it is generally free of any major errors, though there are a number of small mechanical errors.

A Student Essay Scored 4

In the two poems, "Dulce et Decorum Est" and "Old Soldier" a description of war is given but they are quite different. There are many differences between the two poems that can be seen in their point of view, imagery, alliteration, diction, and similes.

First, the poem "Dulce et Decorum Est" describes war from the point of view of a soldier who is actually fighting in the war. The imagery is very vivid and paints a picture in your mind as to what war is really like. The soldiers are "bent double, like old beggars under sacks." He uses many similes as well like "as under a green sea" (line 14) and "bitter as the cud" in (line 23). He also uses alliteration when he says "Knock-kneed, coughing like hags, we cursed through sludge" which repeats the sound of a K. This poem really lets the reader know how horrible war is.

The second poem "Old Soldier" is told from a ten year old boy's view. He is like any other ten year old boy and likes to play "war" all the time. He uses cardboard for a sword and uses his imagination to fight hundreds of battles. The diction in this poem is very positive. He talks about cherry trees, cats lying in the grass, and the horse waving a merry tail. He is just a boy who isn't bothered by the world around him at all. To him war is just play. He doesn't realize how horrible war can really be. These are some of the more important similarities and differences between the two poems.

COMMENT

This essay attempts to analyze the two poems but falls short in both depth of analysis and maturity of writing. The writer lists poetic devices rather than explain why these devices are used and how they affect the meaning in both poems.

were mortared, but it was not battle, it was just the
endless march, village to village, without purpose,
nothing won or lost. They marched for the sake of the
march. They plodded along slowly, dumbly, leaning
forward against the heat, unthinking, all blood and   30
bone, simple grunts, soldiering with their legs, toiling
up the hills and down into the paddies and across the
rivers and up again and down, just humping, one step
and then the next and then another, but no volition, no
will, because it was automatic, it was anatomy, and the   35
war was entirely a matter of posture and carriage, the
hump was everything, a kind of inertia, a kind of
emptiness, a dullness of desire and intellect and
conscience and hope and human sensibility. Their
principles were in their feet. Their calculations were   40
biological. They had no sense of strategy or mission.
They searched the villages without knowing what to
look for, not caring, kicking over jars of rice, frisking
children and old men, blowing tunnels, sometimes
setting fires and sometimes not, then forming up and   45
moving on to the next village, then other villages,
where it would always be the same. They carried their
own lives. The pressures were enormous. In the heat
of early afternoon, they would remove their helmets
and flak jackets, walking bare, which was dangerous   50
but which helped ease the strain. They would often
discard things along the route of march. Purely for
comfort, they would throw away rations, blow their
Claymores and grenades, no matter, because by
nightfall the resupply choppers would arrive with   55
more of the same, then a day or two later still more,
fresh watermelons and crates of ammunition and
sunglasses and woolen sweaters—the resources were
stunning—sparklers for the Fourth of July, colored
eggs for Easter. It was the great American war chest—   60
the fruits of science, the smokestacks, the canneries,
the arsenals at Hartford, the Minnesota forests, the
machine shops, the vast fields of corn and wheat—they
carried like freight trains; they carried it on their backs
and shoulders—and for all the ambiguities of Vietnam,   65
all the mysteries and unknowns, there was at least the
single abiding certainty that they would never be at a
loss for things to carry.

After reading and annotating the passage, compare your annotations with those below.

The following passage is an excerpt from Tim O'Brien's *The Things They Carried*, a novel about life as a soldier during the Vietnam War. Carefully read the passage. Then, in a well-written essay, discuss the complex attitude of the narrator toward the Vietnam War through the author's use of such literary devices as imagery, detail, and syntax.

Soldiers

They carried plastic water containers, each with a two-gallon capacity. Mitchell Sanders carried a set of *odd* starched tiger fatigues for special occasions. Henry Dobbins carried Black Flag insecticide. Dave Jensen carried empty sandbags that would be filled at night   5
for added protection. Lee Strunk carried tanning lotion. Some things they carried in common. Taking *Share* turns, they carried the big PRC-77 scrambler radio, which weighed thirty pounds with its battery. They
? Hmm.... shared the weight of memory. They took up what   10
others could no longer bear. Often, they carried each other, the wounded or weak. They carried infections.
mix of things not They carried chess sets, basketballs, Vietnamese-
normally listed English dictionaries, insignia of rank, Bronze Stars
together and Purple Hearts, plastic cards imprinted with the   15
illness Code of Conduct. They carried diseases, among them malaria and dysentery. They carried lice and
games ringworm and leeches and paddy algae and various
awards rots and molds. They carried the land itself—Vietnam, the place, the soil—a powdery orange-red dust that   20
covered their boots and fatigues and faces. They carried the sky. The whole atmosphere, they carried it, *Place is part of them* the humidity, the monsoons, the stink of fungus and decay, all of it, they carried gravity. They moved like *heavy burden* mules. By daylight they took sniper fire, at night they   25
were mortared, but it was not battle, it was just the endless march, village to village, without purpose, *—no glory* nothing won or lost. They marched for the sake of the *sounds lost or* march. They plodded along slowly, dumbly, leaning *frustrated* forward against the heat, unthinking, all blood and   30
bone, simple grunts, soldiering with their legs, toiling up the hills and down into the paddies and across the
like a robot- rivers and up again and down, just humping, one step
no feelings?! and then the next and then another, but no volition, no will, because it was automatic, it was anatomy, and the   35
war was entirely a matter of posture and carriage, the *looks on outside* hump was everything, a kind of inertia, a kind of emptiness, a dullness of desire and intellect and conscience and hope and human sensibility. Their principles were in their feet. Their calculations were   40
biological. They had no sense of strategy or mission. *animal instinct* They searched the villages without knowing what to

no purpose

look for, <u>not caring</u>, kicking over jars of rice, frisking
children and old men, blowing tunnels, sometimes
setting fires and sometimes not, then forming up and   45
moving on to the next village, then other villages,
where it would always be the same. They carried their
own lives. <u>The pressures were enormous.</u> In the heat   **the pressure of war**
of early afternoon, they would remove their helmets
and flak jackets, walking bare, which was dangerous   50
but which helped ease the strain. They would often
discard things along the route of march. Purely for
comfort, they would throw away rations, blow their   **always have supplies**
Claymores and grenades, no matter, because by
nightfall the resupply choppers would arrive with   55
more of the same, then a day or two later still more,
fresh **?**<u>watermelons</u> and crates of ammunition and   **odd**
<u>sunglasses</u> and <u>woolen sweaters</u>**?**—the resources were   **? Why send**
stunning—<u>sparklers for the Fourth of July</u>, colored
<u>eggs for Easter</u>. It was the great (American war chest)—   60
the fruits of science, the smokestacks, the canneries,   **Whole U.S. industry**
the arsenals at Hartford, the Minnesota forests, the
machine shops, the vast fields of corn and wheat—they
carried like freight trains; they carried it on their backs
and shoulders—and for all the <u>ambiguities of Vietnam</u>,   65
all the mysteries and unknowns, there was at least the
single abiding certainty that <u>they</u> would never be at a
loss for things to carry.   **carry more than "things"—carry**
                                                              emtional baggage

Seems confused by it all.

Planning Your Essay

The essay prompt for Question 2 asks you to determine the attitude of
the narrator toward the war in Vietnam. The prompt tells you that the
passage is about the life of a soldier in Vietnam. As we read the
passage, we notice that the narrator refers to the soldiers as "they";
however, the narrator seems to have intimate knowledge about a
soldier's daily routine and thoughts. The passage is not only about the
objects that each soldier physically carries, but also about the
emotions each soldier carries within. The prompt also tells the reader
that the attitude the narrator has concerning Vietnam is "complex."
The overall purpose of the question is to test your skills in analysis and
interpretation by examining how the details of the passage "echo" the
narrator's view of the war in Vietnam—in particular, the view of an
American soldier in Vietnam. Your task is to determine the narrator's
"complex attitude" toward the war and explain how the use of literary
devices helped create that attitude.

Note that there are no specific literary devices listed in the writing
prompt. This is not to say that prompts for prose analysis don't give
suggested lists; it simply means that *sometimes* they don't. This
prompt simply asks you to identify "literary devices." Be sure to

include those devices that are, in your view, the most important in conveying the author's message.

THE SCORING GUIDELINES

The scoring guidelines, below, follow the concepts and language of the scoring guidelines used by the College Board. To receive a score of 6 or higher, you must successfully respond to the prompt. AP readers score each essay knowing it was composed as a rough draft. Your essay may have mistakes—mistakes are found even in papers scoring a 9. However, an essay with many distracting errors in grammar and mechanics will not be scored higher than a 3.

9–8 Essays in this scoring range illustrate a persuasive, effective, and insightful analysis of how specific literary devices develop the complex attitude of the narrator toward the war in Vietnam. These essays show consistent and effective control of language with writing that is clear, cohesive, and stylistically mature. An essay scoring a 9 is particularly insightful in its interpretation of the passage and uses a sophisticated style appropriate for overall literary analysis.

7–6 Essays in the upper-half range give a reasonable interpretation of the passage and offer an effective analysis of the literary devices used to create the narrator's attitude toward the war. Writers use text evidence to suggest how devices such as point of view, imagery, and punctuation function within the passage. These essays show more consistency in analysis than an essay scored 5 does. Papers scored a 7 exhibit more sophistication in both the effectiveness of their analysis and their overall style.

5 These essays demonstrate an ability to respond to the prompt with an acceptable overall reading of the passage but provide only a superficial analysis. Often these essays show some analysis but then resort to paraphrasing. There is little or no consistency in the development of ideas. These essays may begin to discuss a particular literary device used in the passage but then fail to give an interpretation as to how the device or technique reflects the author's complex attitude toward the war. These essays do show adequate writing skills but are often marred by grammar and punctuation errors. Many times an essay scored a 5 essay will seem formulaic or superficial in its analysis.

4–3 These essays attempt to respond to the prompt but may misinterpret a portion of the passage or fail to develop a cohesive analysis of the passage as a whole. Many essays in this range lack fully developed ideas and resort to paraphrasing the passage rather than analyzing and interpreting it. There is usually a lack of control in some areas of the writing, such as awkward wording and/or problems with punctuation. The essay may be repetitive (saying the same thing over and over). There are few or no textual examples to support any ideas in the essay. An essay score of 3 is given to writing that is particularly simplistic.

2–1 Essays in this range may attempt to answer the prompt but include a serious misreading of the passage or the prompt. They respond to the prompt in a general way, with no specific reference to the passage. These essays may consist of the student's personal views of the Vietnam War, which are separate from the passage. These essays are not well developed in their response to the prompt and lack control in their language. The vocabulary used may be simplistic. These essays fail to show any attempt at analysis and tend to ramble. A score of 1 is given to papers with no development of ideas.

0 An essay that merely repeats the prompt is given a 0.

— This indicates a blank response or the writing was completely off topic.

Sample Student Prose Essays with Comments

A Student Essay Scored 8

One of the most popular authors of the Vietnam War, Tim O'Brien, shows in this passage the myriad of emotions and ideas associated with being a soldier in Vietnam. The narration, in third person and in past tense, uses "they carried" often, suggesting that there is a need to disassociate himself from the action and separate the past and the present. There is a mixture of emotions regarding Vietnam—all represented within various descriptions of what the soldiers carry. There are objects such as "tanning lotion" and "Black Flag insecticide" that are unique to the individual soldier. These individual items characterize the individual personalities, but the focus is on what the soldiers carry in common. What they share with each other. It is a motley list of items that normally do not go together, but in the extreme circumstances of war, they become a part of every soldier. The narrator uses a series of juxtapositions to list the things they carry. There are the wounds of battle carried along with the basketball or the chess set. There are the diseases such as malaria and dysentery mingled with lice and ringworm. The medals of war such as the Purple Heart and the Bronze Star are carried in the same pockets as the dust of Vietnam itself. It is a mixture of courage, stamina, and chance.

The narrator says that the soldiers carry "the whole atmosphere" of Vietnam, which is not seen in a favorable light from the use of imagery provided, "stink of fungus and decay" and the "powdery orange-red dust that covered their boots and fatigues and faces." It seems to be a sort of cursed land to the narrator. Later, the narrator discusses the empty monotony of the soldier's march during the day. The passage is sprinkled with frustration and weariness with "endless march," "without purpose," "nothing won or lost," "dumb," and "unthinking." What is absent is a sense of mission and accomplishment. The narrator does not view the war as an event with a decided purpose. It is a war that is more concerned with appearances than actual realities. He is quick to point out that there is no "sense of strategy or mission" and that the soldiers are functioning more as animals driven by the instinct to survive than by the intellect that man is capable of. The war in all its cruelties has no high purpose, no actual mission to save the world. They are focused on saving themselves. War is an aggressive action that goes against our intellect. He says the "pressures were enormous" that they carried each day. The irony is that the soldiers are given "sparklers for the Fourth of July, colored eggs for Easter," all as part of the American war chest—not gold, medicine, land, glory—all the things we associate with a war chest. The things that are sent to them are not practical, but merely a reminder of the innocence they left behind in a country far away. Despite what each soldier carries, in the end there is no question regarding the fact that the soldier will never have a loss for things to carry. The most important baggage of all is the emotional baggage that each soldier will continue to carry long after the war is over. The end of the passage suggests that as the soldiers go on marching, the war machine of industry keeps on churning out the food and ammunition needed to continue the war. It is the profit of war—a gain of dollars for one and the loss of life for another.

Vietnam becomes a place of "ambiguities" where the narrator points out that at one point they are operating solely on the instinct to survive and the next they are taking off their helmets and jackets, despite the threat of sniper fire, for a reprieve from the heat of the day. The syntax of the passage weaves short statements of fact such as "They moved like mules" with a series of clauses separated by commas. There are no long pauses in the passage that reflect the life of the soldier, for they have no time to rest either. There are scattered thoughts here and there written as dependent clauses, which gives the overall impression of a narrator speaking about his experience in a series of disjointed scenes and thoughts. Everything from the topography of the land to the thinking of the men is described in contrast. Vietnam is not a place only of death, only of frustration, only of a loss of innocence, but a combination of many things including a place of camaraderie. But even the sense of belonging has its price and as the narrator comments "they would never be at a loss for things to carry."

COMMENT

This essay effectively analyzes the passage and discusses the complexity of emotion created by the narrator. The student notes the narrator's point of view, as well as the use of past tense as a means of detachment from a scene that perhaps the author does not want to be a part of. The contrast in objects is noted in the first paragraph of the essay and summed up with "it is a mixture of courage, stamina, and chance." The essay provides examples from the selection and then comments insightfully on their purpose. For example, the student notes the idea that the shipment of "sparklers for the Fourth of July" and "colored eggs for Easter" is especially ironic ; there is no use for either object in Vietnam, and they only serve to remind the soldiers of the innocent traditions of home. The student also comments on the fact that war is a loss of life for the soldier who fights but a boon for industry in providing the weapons of war. The essay does have some problems with wording, but in general, it shows a mature writing style and, more importantly, insightful analysis.

A Student Essay Scored 6

In the passage from <u>The Things They Carried</u>, the narrator reflects a complex attitude toward the war in Vietnam. First, the soldiers are described as carrying an assortment of objects from "tanning lotion" to "ringworm." Some of the objects they carry are positive or useful—like the tanning lotion—but others are not. The objects that the soldiers carry depict the many aspects of Vietnam and the war. Vietnam is a hot country with plenty of sun so it makes sense to carry tanning lotion, plastic water containers, and insecticide; however, there are other objects that are carried that don't make sense such as Sanders' "starched tiger fatigues." Why would you need to starch anything in the jungle? The Vietnam War is viewed through the things the soldiers carry. The war at times seems rational—something that is necessary like the insecticide and at other times completely senseless like the need to carry starched fatigues. The author uses a lot of juxtaposition in that he draws attention to the contrast between items such as the soldiers "carrying" lice and ringworm at the same time they are carrying Bronze Stars and a PRC-77 scrambler radio.

The narrator describes the soldiers as "simple grunts" perhaps incapable of independent thought. They are described as acting out of instinct rather than obeying a set of rational, well-planned orders. The narrator suggests that perhaps the war in Vietnam was based on gut reaction rather than a well thought-out decision. Regardless of the things they will use along the trail, the soldiers will always have something to carry according to the narrator. The American war chest continues to supply what the soldiers need—for practicality purposes but not for their emotional needs. It is the emotional baggage from the war that the soldiers will carry with them forever.

The narrator is torn between the need to do his duty as an American soldier and to justify the reason for why he was there. The items each soldier's pack carried signified bits and pieces of the puzzle known as Vietnam. The experience itself is complex for the narrator for he remembers the feelings of frustration and exhaustion through each item and as fragmented thoughts throughout the passage much like someone who has suffered trauma. Vietnam is a series of images, mostly negative, that are a part of him forever. However, he says that they "carry their own lives" as though each man is the simply the sum of what he carries on his back.

The passage ends with a surreal scene of soldiers taking off their protective gear (flak jackets) and blowing up their ammunition for fun knowing of course that there is plenty of ammo waiting for them at the end of the day. It's as if for that brief period in the heat of the day, their cares are thrown aside. The baggage is tossed away and the war for a little while gets tossed away as well. However, the ending sentence sums up the narrator's view that "there will always be things to carry" whether they are in the farm fields back home or in the rice fields of Vietnam. The experience of Vietnam will always be baggage, a burden, to carry.

COMMENT

This is a developed essay that does an effective job of analyzing the text and explaining how the literary devices used (juxtaposition, diction) contribute to the narrator's view of the Vietnam War. The sentence structure is varied, and the control of language is apparent; however, the writing is generally unsophisticated in style and diction. The student does understand the connection between the objects carried by the soldiers and their relation to the attitude the narrator has for the war itself.

A Student Essay Scored 4

The soldiers in the passage <u>The Things They Carried</u> reflect the attitude of the narrator. The narrator describes many things that the soldiers are carrying including tanning lotion, empty sandbags, insecticide. They also carry lice, ringworm, and other infectious diseases. The soldiers carry a lot of different things just like the narrator thinks about the Vietnam War. He talks about Vietnam as having monsoons, orange-red dust, stink of fungus and having the people live in villages. Vietnam seems to be a very unpleasant place for the narrator. The narrator also describes the American soldiers as being "unthinking" and "all blood and bone, simple grunts." He doesn't think too highly of the American soldiers because they are only acting on instincts and the war is an example of the "dullness of desire and intellect and conscience and hope and human sensibility." He then goes on to say that the soldiers had enormous pressure on them (line 48). The pressure of course came from the struggle to survive with the threat of sniper fire and mortars. Later in the passage the narrator speaks about the American war chest and how it was full of different things like colored Easter eggs, sparklers, woolen sweaters, sunglasses, and watermelons. The items in the war chest were not practical items except for the ammunition. The reader wonders why such items would be sent to the soldiers in Vietnam which leads you to think about why America sent soldiers to Vietnam. Perhaps both were impractical. In any case, the narrator sees the war in many different ways both dangerous and without purpose.

A Sample Open Essay Question

Question 3

"When the world goes mad, one must accept madness as sanity; since sanity is, in the last analysis, nothing but the madness on which the whole world happens to agree."
—George Bernard Shaw (1856–1950)

Select a novel or play in which a character or a situation of "madness" plays an important role. In a well-written essay, explain how the madness is manifested and why it is important to the work as a whole. Then explain how such madness could be viewed as something "on which the whole world happens to agree." You may select a work from the list below or choose another novel or play of literary merit.

1984	*Hamlet*
A Doll House	*Heart of Darkness*
A Streetcar Named Desire	*Les Misérables*
A Tale of Two Cities	*One Flew over the Cuckoo's Nest*
An Enemy of the People	*Sula*
As I Lay Dying	*The Awakening*
Beloved	*The Color Purple*
Brave New World	*The Crucible*
Catch-22	*The Grapes of Wrath*
Catcher in the Rye	*The Things They Carried*
Crime and Punishment	*Their Eyes Were Watching God*
Death of a Salesman	*The Red Badge of Courage*
Fahrenheit 451	*Things Fall Apart*

PLANNING YOUR ESSAY

This prompt begins with a quote by George Bernard Shaw as a way to jump-start ideas about what the words "madness" and "sanity" mean. When there is a quote at the beginning of your open-essay prompt, read it carefully and try to paraphrase it so that it makes sense to you before attempting to begin your essay. Here Shaw says that when the world goes mad, it is no longer viewed as madness, but becomes sanity, an accepted practice or behavior. What was once considered strange behavior or thought becomes ordinary or acceptable. However, Shaw goes on to say that what society considers sane is really madness that society has come to accept or agree upon.

After you have wrapped your thoughts around the quote, it is time to look at the prompt itself. What is the prompt asking you to do? The prompt calls for an essay based on a work in which "madness" is fundamental, either to the development of a character or to the construction of the plot. Think about novels you have read that deal with madness or insanity. You can write about a work of your choosing, but the list accompanying a Question 3 prompt is worth looking at closely. It may contain a novel or play you are familiar with but had simply forgotten.

Be sure to answer the *entire* prompt—essential for an upper-level score. This prompt has several parts. First, you are asked to describe the madness of a character or situation and how the author uses it. Then you are asked to "explain how such madness could be viewed as something 'on which the whole world happens to agree.'" Did the world or the characters in the novel or play for the most part begin to support the madness or begin to accept the madness as appropriate behavior or sane? Notice that the prompt uses the verb "could be viewed" rather than "was viewed." The characters in the novel or play you choose may not have embraced the madness as sanity, but in what way could the madness be seen as an act of sanity? You will need to discuss how the madness was actually viewed in the literature you selected and then briefly discuss how the madness could have been accepted as a sane act or thought.

THE SCORING GUIDELINES

The scoring guidelines, below, follow the concepts and language of the scoring guidelines used by the College Board. To receive a score of 6 or higher, you must successfully respond to the prompt. AP readers score each essay knowing it was composed as a rough draft. Your essay may have mistakes—mistakes are found even in papers scoring a 9. However, an essay with many distracting errors in grammar and mechanics will not be scored higher than a 3.

9–8 Essays in this scoring range illustrate a persuasive, effective, and insightful analysis of "madness" or the irrational behavior of a character in an appropriate novel or play. They explain the specific "madness" in the literary work, as well as how it's developed. Furthermore, they show how the madness might be judged reasonable by others in the context of the work. These essays show consistent and effective control of language. Writing is clear, cohesive, and mature in are able to be individuals by the end of the story and taste freedom along with being able to drink beer and have prostitutes. He is able to turn them in to men again.

In <u>One Flew over the Cuckoo's Nest</u>, McMurphy is said to be crazy. He proves that this is not true, and because of his so called "symptoms" he cures the entire mental ward. McMurphy plays a important role in this novel by helping to take away some of Nurse Ratched's power and give it to the patients.

COMMENT

The essay begins by explaining why McMurphy is seen as "mad" by general society; however, the essay does not analyze the reasons why the main character chooses to act as he does, other than to say it was "either that or prison." The connection between McMurphy's behavior and individuality is loose. The essay tends to summarize the plot of the story more than answer questions of how McMurphy's actions could be justified beyond saying "[a] lot of people drink too much." It also doesn't connect McMurphy's actions to a greater theme in the novel. The essay hints at "freedom" and "individuality" but doesn't connect them clearly to McMurphy's supposed "madness." The language is limited and there are a number of spelling and other grammatical errors.

Part III

Practice Tests

PRACTICE TEST 1

AP ENGLISH LITERATURE AND COMPOSITION EXAMINATION
Section I: Multiple-Choice Questions
Number of questions: 55
Total time: 1 hour

DIRECTIONS: This part consists of selections from literary works and questions on their content, form, and style. After reading each passage, choose the best answer to the accompanying questions.

QUESTIONS 1–11. Carefully read the passage, the opening of the short story "Civil Peace" by Chinua Achebe, before choosing your answers.

Jonathan Iwegbu counted himself extraordinarily lucky. "Happy survival!" meant so much more to him than just a current fashion of greeting old friends in the first hazy days of peace. It went deep to his heart. He had come out of the war with five inestimable blessings— his head, his wife Maria's head, and the heads of three out of their four 5 children. As a bonus he also had his old bicycle—a miracle too but naturally not to be compared to the safety of five human heads.

The bicycle had a little history of its own. One day at the height of the war it was commandeered "for urgent military action." Hard as its loss would have been to him he would still have let it go without a 10 thought had he not had some doubts about the genuineness of the officer. It wasn't his disreputable table rags, nor the toes peeping out of one blue and one brown canvas shoes, nor yet the two stars of his rank done obviously in a hurry in biro,[1] that troubled Jonathan; many good and heroic soldiers looked the same or worse. It was rather a certain 15 lack of grip and firmness in his manner. So Jonathan, suspecting he might be amenable to influence, rummaged in his raffia bag and produced the two pounds with which he had been going to buy firewood which his wife, Maria, retailed to camp officials for extra stock-fish and corn meal, and got his bicycle back. That night he buried 20 it in the little clearing in the bush where the dead of the camp, including his own youngest son, were buried. When he dug it up again a year later after the surrender all it needed was a little palm-oil greasing. "Nothing puzzles God," he said in wonder.

He put it to immediate use as a taxi and accumulated a small pile of 25 Biafran money ferrying camp officials and their families across the four- mile stretch to the nearest tarred road. His standard charge per trip was six pounds and those who had the money were only glad to be rid of some of it in this way. At the end of a fortnight he had made a small fortune of one hundred and fifteen pounds. 30

---

[1] A ball-point pen.

GO ON TO THE NEXT PAGE

Then he made the journey to Enugu and found another miracle waiting for him. It was unbelievable. He rubbed his eyes and looked again and it was still standing there before him. But, needless to say, even that monumental blessing must be accounted also totally inferior to the five heads in the family. This newest miracle was his little house   35
in Ogui Overside. Indeed nothing puzzles God! Only two houses away a huge concrete edifice some wealthy contractor had put up just before the war was a mountain of rubble. And here was Jonathan's little zinc house of no regrets built with mud blocks quite intact! Of course the doors and windows were missing and five sheets off the roof. But what   40
was that? And anyhow he had returned to Enugu early enough to pick up bits of old zinc and wood and soggy sheets of cardboard lying around the neighborhood before thousands more came out of their forest holes looking for the same things. He got a destitute carpenter with one old hammer, a blunt plane, and a few bent and rusty nails in   45
his tool bag to turn this assortment of wood, paper, and metal into door and window shutters for five Nigerian shillings or fifty Biafran pounds. He paid the pounds, and moved in with his overjoyed family carrying five heads on their shoulders.

His children picked mangoes near the military cemetery and sold   50
them to soldiers' wives for a few pennies—real pennies this time—and his wife started making breakfast akara balls for neighbors in a hurry to start life again. With his family earnings he took his bicycle to the villages around and bought fresh palm-wine which he mixed generously in his rooms with the water which had recently started   55
running again in the public tap down the road, and opened up a bar for soldiers and other lucky people with good money.

At first he went daily, then every other day, and finally once a week, to the offices of the Coal Corporation where he used to be a miner, to find out what was what. The only thing he did find out in the   60
end was that that little house of his was even a greater blessing than he had thought. Some of his fellow ex-miners who had nowhere to return at the end of the day's waiting just slept outside the doors of the offices and cooked what meal they could scrounge together in Bournvita tins. As the weeks lengthened and still nobody could say what was what   65
Jonathan discontinued his weekly visits altogether and faced his palm-wine bar.

1. The description of the officer (lines 12–16) helps to convey all of the following EXCEPT
    (A) the irregular nature of the armed forces
    (B) the poverty of the country facing the civil war
    (C) a sense of the noble incorruptibility of even the most ordinary citizen
    (D) a compassionate undertone of humor
    (E) the real reason for Jonathan's uneasiness with the officer

2. From the characterization of the officer as "amenable to influence" (line 17), we can infer that
    (A) he is easily led to drink to excess
    (B) he can be persuaded to change sides in the civil war
    (C) he has pull with the owners of the mines
    (D) Jonathan wants to avoid him to protect his family
    (E) he can be bribed

3. The narrator most likely limits the account of the death of Jonathan's youngest son to two short phrases in order to
   (A) emphasize Jonathan's refusal to let a deeply felt tragedy defeat him
   (B) avoid letting this one detail overshadow the real meaning of the passage
   (C) suggest that the death is less important to Jonathan because he has three other children
   (D) foreshadow the finding of the little house in Ogui Overside
   (E) echo the other children's picking "mangoes near the military cemetery" (line 50)

4. In the context of the story, the repeated phrase "nothing puzzles God" is best interpreted to mean that, for Jonathan,
   (A) God is mystified that some humans send nothing in prayer to Heaven
   (B) there is no way to fool God, even though some people like to try
   (C) God will reward the righteous and punish the unfaithful
   (D) God is in control, even though humans may be perplexed by happenings in life
   (E) God trusts humans to work out their own difficulties

5. The most obvious example of irony in the passage concerns
   (A) the colors of the officer's shoes (line 13)
   (B) Jonathan's charging the camp officials six pounds per trip (line 28)
   (C) Jonathan's finding a "destitute carpenter" to repair the house (line 44)
   (D) the "little house" in Ogui Overside surviving the war (lines 35–38)
   (E) the water's starting to run again in the public tap (lines 55–56)

6. In the context of the passage, the sentence "But what was that?" (lines 40–41) is best understood to mean that Jonathan has
   (A) heard a noise he can't identify
   (B) renewed resilience in spite of setbacks
   (C) seen the "five sheets" in the distance
   (D) forgotten what he was looking for
   (E) heard others arriving to threaten his house

7. Which of the following lines offers an example of synecdoche?
   (A) line 5
   (B) line 9
   (C) lines 19–20
   (D) lines 31–32
   (E) lines 50–51

8. The people in the passage are characterized chiefly by description of their
   (A) clothes and belongings
   (B) thoughts
   (C) dialogue with each other
   (D) actions
   (E) dreams and hopes

9. The style of the passage as a whole is best described as
   (A) metaphorical and ornate
   (B) convoluted and intricate
   (C) cerebral and pedantic
   (D) incredulous and skeptical
   (E) direct and simple

10. The narrator's attitude toward Jonathan is best characterized as one of
    (A) condescension but understanding
    (B) sympathy, pity, and sorrow
    (C) warmth, respect, and admiration
    (D) soft censure and mild rebuke
    (E) indifference except as he can serve as a metaphor

GO ON TO THE NEXT PAGE

11. The passage as a whole is best
    described as a(n)
    (A) narrative definition of the horrors
       of war
    (B) clarification of the relationship
       among the members of the family
    (C) presentation of a philosophical
       opposition to civil war
    (D) presentation of a political
       opposition to civil war
    (E) extended confirmation of the
       passage's opening sentence

QUESTIONS 12–22. Carefully read "One day I wrote her name upon the strand" by Edmund
Spenser before choosing your answers.

> One day I wrote her name upon the strand,
> But came the waves and washèd it away:
> Again I wrote it with a second hand,
> But came the tide, and made my pains his prey.
> "Vain man," said she, "that dost in vain assay   5
> A mortal thing so to immortalize.
> For I myself shall, like to this, decay,
> And eek[2] my name be wipèd out likewise."
> "Not so," quoth I, "let baser things devise
> To die in dust, but you shall live by fame: 10
> My verse your virtues rare shall eternize,
> And in the heavens write your glorious name,
> Where whenas death shall all the world subdue
> Our love shall live, and later life renew."

12. The speaker in the poem is
    (A) a heavenly spirit
    (B) a lifeguard
    (C) a poet in love
    (D) a religious leader
    (E) a passing stranger

13. The phrase "came the tide, and made
    my pains his prey" (line 4) is best
    interpreted to mean
    (A) the tide wiped out all my hard
       work
    (B) the tide caught me and caused me
       physical pain
    (C) the water temporarily alleviated
       my emotional pains
    (D) history turned against all my best
       intentions
    (E) the heavens would not hear my
       prayer

14. The poet begins line 5 with the word
    "vain" in order to
    I. set up the pun on the same word
       later in the line
    II. allow the woman to gently mock
       the speaker's claim
    III. introduce the main idea of the
       poem's second quatrain
    (A) I only
    (B) I and II only
    (C) I and III only
    (D) II and III only
    (E) I ,II, and III

---

[2] Also.

15. The pronoun "she" in line 5 refers to the same person as
(A) the strand (line 1)
(B) "her" (line 1)
(C) the name (line 1)
(D) the tide (line 4)
(E) the prey (line 4)

16. When "she" says "I myself shall, like to this, decay" (line 7), by "this" she means
(A) the relationship between the speaker and herself
(B) the verse the speaker has constructed
(C) the speaker's own death
(D) her name, which the speaker has written in the sand
(E) the pains the speaker has taken on her behalf

17. By "my name" (line 8) the woman means
(A) earthly memory of her
(B) her good reputation
(C) her earthly life
(D) her physical beauty
(E) her moral character

18. The speaker's attitude toward his "verse" (line 11) is best characterized as
(A) intensely ashamed
(B) insecurely hesitant
(C) coolly distant
(D) wholly confident
(E) quietly content

19. All of the following are true of line 14 EXCEPT
(A) it introduces a striking new idea into the poem
(B) the rhythm is quickened by the alliterative "L"s
(C) it is true, since we are still reading the poem today
(D) it completes the rhyming couplet begun by line 13
(E) the speaker uses it to close his argument with a promise

20. The two clear shifts in the poem come after lines
(A) 2 and 10
(B) 4 and 8
(C) 4 and 10
(D) 4 and 12
(E) 8 and 12

21. The tone of the speaker in the poem is best described as
(A) wistful and nostalgic
(B) frustrated and disappointed
(C) jocund and sardonic
(D) incredulous and scornful
(E) reassuring and secure

22. The lines that best state the main idea of the poem are
(A) 1 and 2
(B) 1 and 3
(C) 5 and 6
(D) 7 and 8
(E) 11 and 14

GO ON TO THE NEXT PAGE

QUESTIONS 23–33. Carefully read the poem by Philip Larkin before choosing your answers.

Aubade

I work all day, and get half drunk at night.
Waking at four to soundless dark, I stare.
In time the curtain-edges will grow light.
Till then I see what's really always there:
Unresting death, a whole day nearer now,   5
Making all thought impossible but how
And where and when I shall myself die.
Arid interrogation: yet the dread
Of dying, and being dead,
Flashes afresh to hold and horrify.   10

The mind blanks at the glare. Not in remorse
—The good not done, the love not given, time
Torn off unused—nor wretchedly because
An only life can take so long to climb
Clear of its wrong beginnings, and may never;   15
But at the total emptiness for ever,
The sure extinction that we travel to
And shall be lost in always. Not to be here,
Not to be anywhere,
And soon; nothing more terrible, nothing more true.   20

This is a special way of being afraid
No trick dispels. Religion used to try,
That vast moth-eaten musical brocade
Created to pretend we never die,
And specious stuff that says *No rational being*   25
Can fear a thing it will not feel, not seeing
That this is what we fear—no sight, no sound,
No touch or taste or smell, nothing to think with,
Nothing to love or link with,
The anaesthetic from which none come round.   30

And so it stays just on the edge of vision,
A small unfocused blur, a standing chill
That slows each impulse down to indecision.
Most things may never happen: this one will,
And realization of it rages out   35
In furnace-fear when we are caught without
People or drink. Courage is no good:
It means not scaring others. Being brave
Lets no one off the grave.
Death is no different whined at than withstood.   40

Slowly light strengthens, and the room takes shape.
It stands plain as a wardrobe, what we know,
Have always known, know that we can't escape,
Yet can't accept. One side will have to go.

Meanwhile telephones crouch, getting ready to ring   45
In locked-up offices, and all the uncaring
Intricate rented world begins to rouse.
The sky is white as clay, with no sun.
Work has to be done.
Postmen like doctors go from house to house.   50

23. The speaker in this poem is best identified as
    (A) a man who has been taken into police custody for drunkenness
    (B) a man who awakens in his bedroom during the night
    (C) a man who awakens in a frightening, unfamiliar place
    (D) a patient who awakens in a hospital critical care unit
    (E) a doctor who has risen early to make house calls to his dying patients

24. The phrase "arid interrogation" in line 8 is best understood to mean that the speaker
    (A) cannot speak the answers because of "dry mouth" caused by medication
    (B) fears he will not have answers for the questions at the Last Judgment
    (C) is dehydrated from alcohol abuse
    (D) knows he can't find answers to his questions
    (E) has awoken in his bed with "night sweats"

25. Which of the following best identifies the source of the "glare" in line 11?
    (A) "the curtain-edges" that "grow light" (line 3)
    (B) "dying, and being dead" (line 9)
    (C) "the dread of dying" (lines 8–9)
    (D) the "[a]rid interrogation" (line 8)
    (E) the "[m]aking all thought impossible" (line 6)

26. The poet uses the phrases "The good not done, the love not given, time / Torn off unused" (lines 12–13) to
    (A) contradict the idea expressed by "the dread / Of dying" (lines 8–9)
    (B) enumerate some of the causes of the potential "remorse" (line 11)

    (C) contrast with the thought of "[m]aking all thought impossible" (line 6)
    (D) foreshadow the "wrong beginnings" of life (line 15)
    (E) provide examples of actions that "hold and horrify" (line 10)

27. Which of the following is implicit after the phrase "may never" in line 15?
    (A) "die" (line 7)
    (B) "[t]orn off unused" (line 13)
    (C) "take so long" (line 14)
    (D) "climb / Clear of its wrong beginnings" (lines 14–15)
    (E) "travel to" [extinction] (line 17)

28. Which of the following best identifies what the speaker calls "terrible" and "true" in line 20?
    (A) "love not given" (line 12)
    (B) life taking "so long" (line 14)
    (C) "wrong beginnings" (line 15)
    (D) the "good not done" (line 12)
    (E) "Not to be anywhere" (line 19)

29. In the context of the poem, the phrase "moth-eaten musical brocade" (line 23) is intended to suggest all of the following EXCEPT
    (A) rich opulence
    (B) elaborateness
    (C) heaviness
    (D) the natural world
    (E) ineffectiveness

30. Which of the following best paraphrases line 33?
    (A) that makes our bodies incapable of responding to external stimuli
    (B) that draws us, in spite of our efforts, toward our deaths
    (C) that helps us make up our minds to move slowly and surely
    (D) that suppresses our impulses but also increases our momentum
    (E) that robs us of the emotional stamina to perform our duties

GO ON TO THE NEXT PAGE

31. One purpose of line 40 is to
    (A) reinforce the idea that being brave when faced with death is meaningless
    (B) suggest that resisting and even complaining when death threatens can bring strength
    (C) counter the argument that "Being brave / Lets no one off the grave" (lines 38–39)
    (D) assert again that religion teaches us how to avoid whining when faced with death
    (E) present a metaphor that helps makes sense of death

32. The diction in line 45 suggests that the speaker sees telephones as
    (A) an aggressive presence that stalks humans
    (B) a reassuring metaphor for the link between humans and the divine
    (C) a comforting symbol of the return to calm normalcy after the fears of the night
    (D) a mechanical piece of an indifferent daily life of routine
    (E) a call to action against "all the uncaring" world

33. An aubade is a song or poem greeting the dawn, a morning love song, or a poem about the parting of lovers at dawn, so its use as the title here brings to the poem
    (A) a softening reassurance
    (B) a lyrical intensity
    (C) a climactic culmination
    (D) a mordant irony
    (E) a promise of hope

QUESTIONS 34–44. The following is an excerpt from the first act of *Tartuffe* by Molière. Orgon, a wealthy gentleman, has invited Tartuffe, who poses as deeply religious, into his home. Here he returns home and talks with Dorine, a lady's maid to his daughter and his brother-in-law Cléante. Carefully read the passage before choosing your answers.

SCENE 4
(Enter ORGON [who discovers CLÉANTE and DORINE])
ORGON. Ah, Brother, good-day.
CLÉANTE. Well, welcome back. I'm sorry I can't stay.
　　How was the country? Blooming, I trust, and green?
ORGON. Excuse me, Brother; just one moment.　　　　　　　　　5
　　(to DORINE) Dorine . . .
　　(to CLÉANTE) To put my mind at rest, I always learn
　　The household news the moment I return.
　　(to DORINE) Has all been well, these two days I've been gone?
　　How are the family? What's been going on?　　　　　　　　10
DORINE. Your wife, two days ago, had a bad fever,
　　And a fierce headache which refused to leave her.
ORGON. Ah. And Tartuffe?
DORINE. Tartuffe? Why, he's round and red,　　　　　　　　　15
　　Bursting with health, and excellently fed.
ORGON. Poor fellow!
DORINE. That night, the mistress was unable
　　To take a single bite at the dinner-table.
　　Her headache-pains, she said, were simply hellish.
ORGON. Ah. And Tartuffe?　　　　　　　　　　　　　　　　　20
DORINE. He ate his meal with relish,
　　And zealously devoured in her presence
　　A leg of mutton and a brace of pheasants.
ORGON. Poor fellow!
DORINE. Well, the pains continued strong,　　　　　　　　　25
　　And so she tossed and tossed the whole night long,
　　Now icy-cold, now burning like a flame.
　　We sat beside her bed till morning came.

48. The speaker's statement that "the woman borrowed my grandmother's face" (line 10) is best understood to mean that
    (A) to identify with the old woman in line 5, the speaker as a child needed to picture her own grandmother in her place
    (B) the speaker is angry that her choice was made difficult by the resemblance of the old woman in line 5 to her grandmother
    (C) the speaker feels fortunate that the painter would use her own grandmother as a model
    (D) the teacher would try to get her students to take the assignment seriously by calling up their memories of their grandparents
    (E) the lighting in the museum made the woman in the painting look like the speaker's own grandmother

49. The diction in the teacher's response to the suggestion of letting "the old woman decide herself" (line 14) carries a tone of
    (A) unforgiving and severe censure
    (B) mocking but mild reproach
    (C) rueful but nostalgic regret
    (D) untroubled but aloof indifference
    (E) vehement but poignant anger

50. The phrase "old woman" in line 18 refers to
    (A) the woman in the painting by Rembrandt
    (B) the teacher
    (C) a museum guard or docent
    (D) an anonymous painter
    (E) the speaker herself

51. The seasons autumn and winter in the context of lines 20–21 are best understood to suggest
    (A) aging and death
    (B) the children and the old woman
    (C) holidays and festivals
    (D) the carelessness of humans toward the environment
    (E) the museum as shelter from rough weather

52. The most significant shift in the poem comes
    (A) in line 9
    (B) between lines 12 and 13
    (C) between lines 16 and 17
    (D) in line 19
    (E) in line 23

53. The tone that prevails throughout the poem is best characterized as
    (A) wistful and nostalgic
    (B) whimsical and mischievous
    (C) pessimistic and suspicious
    (D) mournful and crestfallen
    (E) reflective and realistic

54. The speaker most closely identifies with
    (A) the teacher (line 2)
    (B) the woman in the "Rembrandt painting" (line 4)
    (C) the "old woman who hadn't many / years left anyhow" (lines 5–6)
    (D) the children, "[r]estless on hard chairs" (line 6)
    (E) her grandmother (line 10)

55. The poem as a whole implies that "all [are] beyond saving by children" for all the following reasons EXCEPT
    (A) children are more immediately concerned with their own physical comfort than with questions of ethics and values
    (B) children are like the girl Linda in lines 15–16, who "eschews / the burdens of responsibility"
    (C) children make ethical decisions at random
    (D) children are closer to "the browns of earth" (line 21) than the older people and more interested in the seasons than in art
    (E) children lack the maturity and the experience to understand the value of the "woman and painting and season" (lines 23–24)

STOP
END OF SECTION I

Section II: Essay Questions
Number of questions: 3
Reading time: 15 minutes
Writing time: 2 hours
Suggested time for each essay: 40 minutes

Section II of this examination requires answers in essay form. Each question counts for one-third of the total essay section score. The two hours are yours to divide among the three essay questions as you think best. To help you use your time well, the proctor may announce the time at which each question should be completed. If you finish any question before time is announced, you may go on to another question. You may go back at any time and work on any essay question you want.

Each essay will be judged on its clarity and effectiveness in dealing with the assigned topic and on the quality of the writing. In response to Question 3, select a work of recognized literary merit appropriate to the question. A good general rule is to use works of the same quality as those you studied in your Advanced Placement literature course(s).

After completing each question, you should check your essay for accuracy of punctuation, spelling, and diction; you are advised, however, not to attempt many longer corrections. Remember that quality is far more important than quantity.

Write your essays clearly and legibly in dark-blue or black ink. Cross out any errors you make.

9. ANSWER: E. *A style question.* Direct and simple matches the content—the account of a straightforward, uncomplicated man. The language is almost without figurative speech; it's a straight, literal narrative. An elegance pervades the writing, but the syntax and the vocabulary are uncomplicated, the opposite of choice B. When choices list two elements, both must be correct for the choice to be the right answer. In A, neither is correct; the piece is nearly without metaphor, and the simplicity eliminates "ornate." C cannot be right because it contradicts the simplicity of tone and naturalness of language. D fails because the optimism in the face of renewed hardships cancels out any skepticism.

10. ANSWER: C. *A question of character and tone.* The narrator's compassion shows in his twice mentioning the death of the son. His admiration shows as in each paragraph he presents another example of Jonathan's diligence and resourcefulness. Choice A gets it half right; there is understanding. But there's no condescension, and half right on a test like this is all wrong. B starts well; there is sympathy in the account, but no pity for a character who would reject it if it came. The "rebuke" eliminates D, and E is incorrect in both parts.

11. ANSWER: E. *A question of meaning and structure.* Each paragraph focuses on one example of what Jonathan would call his luck, and what the narrator presents as a combination of good fortune and Jonathan's own industry. First, he hits on an alleged "officer" who can be bribed, and he moves quickly to save his bicycle. Second, the value of Biafran money falls and he makes a profit with his taxi. Third, he finds his house still standing and a carpenter hungry enough to repair it. Fourth, his family finds buyers for the food they gather or prepare, allowing him to start up his bar. Finally, he sees his former co-workers homeless and hungry when he is neither. Choices A, C, and D are wrong because the passage does not take a stand on the war—in fact, it never explicitly identifies it. An argument can be made that "the horrors of war" in A underlie most of the misfortune the passage shows, but the piece does not show us those horrors, and choice E is more consistent with the positive tone of the passage as a whole.

12. ANSWER: C. *A speaker question—a common type, especially with poetry.* The speaker is a poet who has written "verse." Choice E has no basis in the poem. A and D may appear linked to the mention of "heavens" in the poem, but they have no such link to the speaker. Choice B might sound connected to the beach setting, but it can be quickly eliminated.

13. ANSWER: A. *An interpretation question.* What the tide "preys" on, or destroys, is what the speaker has taken pains to write in the sand. Nothing in the poem supports the idea that he is in any physical or emotional pain, eliminating B and C, and D and E stray even further from the poem.

14. **ANSWER: E.** *A diction question.* Beware of the trap of letting a "Roman numeral question" eat up too much of your time. Their form is complex, but they tend to be somewhat straightforward. Here, I is true since the word means conceited or foolish in the first mention and useless in the phrase "in vain." II is true because the woman teases the speaker by pointing out that her name in the sand is gone and that she, too, will die. Since the second quatrain presents that idea, that the speaker is foolish to think he can fight nature, III is also correct.

15. **ANSWER: B.** *A grammar question.* The woman whose name the speaker writes is the only woman in the poem, so B is the quick choice. C doesn't make sense because "she" is the speaker (or at least the one being quoted) in lines 5–8, and "the name" would not say "my name be wiped out." E won't work for the same reason because "prey" also refers to the name in the sand. We can eliminate A and D since it makes no sense for either the strand or the tide to speak of its own decay.

16. **ANSWER: D.** *A grammar question.* What has decayed in the poem is the name written in the sand. A and C find no support in the poem, and B fails because the speaker claims that the verse will not decay. E sounds acceptable at first, but it is a less satisfying choice than D because the speaker may have taken the pains on her behalf, but more likely did so on his own.

17. **ANSWER: A.** *An interpretation question.* The woman can only mean her name in the sense of records of her and her life. Nothing in the poem has established that she has a good reputation, beauty, or moral character to have wiped out, so B, D, and E don't work. C is a possible choice, but she has already said she will decay like the name in the sand—that is, completely—so C would be simply a restatement. A adds the idea that not only will she die, but the world will forget her after she does so.

18. **ANSWER: D.** *A question of tone and attitude.* The speaker argues resolutely that his poetry will make the woman immortal—maybe a huge claim, but he makes it. B is wrong because there is no insecurity about him. A and E don't work because there's no shame in his tone and nothing quiet about the way he brags about his verse. C is wrong because he seems intent on breaking down *her* distance, not adding his own.

19. **ANSWER: A.** *A question of structure and interpretation.* Poems, especially sonnets, do not introduce new ideas in a final line. "L" sounds—as "liquid sounds"—do speed up a line, the line does form a couplet with line 13, and the speaker promises that their love will outlast mortal life. Even C is true; he was right.

20. **ANSWER: B.** *A structure question.* Punctuation is the easiest clue here; end stops finish lines 4 and 8 and no others. That first shift marks the move from the speaker's vain attempt and the tide's destruction to the new idea—the woman's belief that people don't last forever either. Line 9 then shifts to the speaker's counter-argument that he can make her last forever through his poetry. The rhyme helps some; it does change after line 4 and after line 8, but also after line 12. The shift in speaker reinforces the choice of B since the man speaks lines 1–4, he quotes the woman in 5–8, and returns to his own voice for 9–14.

21. **ANSWER: E.** *A tone question.* The word "secure" leads to E, and "reassuring" may understate the speaker's intent but it is accurate. The "scornful" in D might be tempting if we take it to mean scornful of the earthly decay he claims to be surmounting (probably not what the question means), but "incredulous" clearly does not fit. A weak argument might be made that he's disappointed, but B is wrong because he is certainly not frustrated. As the bold "Not so" shows, he's well prepared with his counter-argument. The others are not supported by any details from the poem.

22. **ANSWER: E.** *A "main idea" question—a very common type.* Since we're looking for two lines that "state the main idea," we need two lines that come close to saying the same thing. Since line 11 says "My poem will make you immortal" and line 14 says "Our love will be immortal," we have a close match. Another clue is that the "main idea" of a sonnet nearly always comes in the closing quatrain or sestet, not near the start.

23. **ANSWER: B.** *A speaker question.* The speaker is normally identified early in a poem. Here the word "I" alerts us, and in the second line we get the answer. The other choices echo words or ideas found in the poem, but in other contexts.

24. **ANSWER: D.** *An interpretation question.* The speaker cannot find the answers to his questions in the previous line, where and when he will die. Choices A, C, and E all appeal to the literal meaning of "arid," but the meaning here is metaphorical. B is not supported by the poem.

25. **ANSWER: C.** *An interpretation question.* The "glare" here comes from the "flashes," and what flashes is the "dread of dying." Choice A picks up on the idea of light, since light glares, but here it's in a different context. The other choices are not supported by details in the poem.

26. **ANSWER: B.** *An interpretation question.* All three phrases are examples of wasted opportunities that bring feelings of remorse. That remorse adds to, rather than lessens, the "dread of dying," so A is wrong. C won't work because it's the death in line 5 that "makes all thought impossible." D is wrong because of logic: actions done or not done during life can't foreshadow its beginnings. E is the best of the wrong choices, but grammatically it can't work because what "hold and horrify" are the flashes of the dread in line 8.

27. ANSWER: D. *A question of grammar and interpretation.* The semicolon at the end of line 25 indicates the end of a grammatical unit, so we have to back up to find what it refers to. The other choices make no grammatical sense

28. ANSWER: E. *A question of grammar and interpretation.* Unless there's strong evidence that we should look elsewhere, we stay in the same sentence to find grammatical relationships. So what's "terrible and true" here is the idea of not being at all. The context supports this choice as well, since the speaker has established that what he dreads is dying and disappearing. The other choices are too far away—both grammatically and in meaning.

29. ANSWER: D. *An interpretation question.* The natural world is far from the speaker's ideas about religion. All the others fit. Brocade is a heavy, rich silk fabric ornamented in gold, eliminating A, B, and C. "Moth-eaten" eliminates E.

30. ANSWER: E. *A reading and paraphrase question.* The line is nearly literal: the fear of death becomes a blur that undoes our impulses and leave us incapable of taking any action. D starts well but then reverses itself. C has a positive tone that the poem does not support, and A mistakes a psychological meaning for a physical one. B makes little sense.

31. ANSWER: A. *A paraphrase question.* The line means that our reaction to death has no effect on it. None of the other choices are supported by the poem; C is contradicted by it.

32. ANSWER: A. *A diction question.* The words "crouch, getting ready" are normally used to describe predatory animals. Choices B, C, and D contradict that image, and E misreads the poem as calling for action. The poem simply laments what it sees as a demoralizing reality.

33. ANSWER: D. *A question of diction and tone.* Since the poem contradicts every element in the definition of aubade, its use in the title here is ironic. Choices A and E represent a serious misreading of this bleak poem, and C does not specify what is being concluded. B is the best of the wrong choices because the poem is certainly intense; the lyricism, however, is not the lyricism implied by the definition of aubade.

34. ANSWER: E. *A question of comic intent.* Since the intention here is clearly comic, only A and E will fit. Orgon's answers are the inappropriate responses of a machine, not those of a thinking human. A may be true, but its observation is irrelevant. Whether Tartuffe is or is not on stage is of no importance.

35. ANSWER: A. *A plot question.* We know from Dorine's answers what Tartuffe has been doing. The other choices make up a list of what we would have expected him to do. (Questions like this one, whose answers are explicit in the text, are unusual.)

36. **ANSWER: C.** *An interpretation question.* In each case, Orgon's wife's conditions worsens, from being ill, to being in "hellish" pain, to being bedridden, and finally to having doctors bleed her—probably with leeches. So each time, Orgon's concern for the healthy and well-fed Tartuffe becomes more out of place. A represents the opposite of the answer. B and E contradict the text, and D has no support in the passage.

37. **ANSWER: C.** *A tone question.* Dorine says she will tell Orgon's wife that he has expressed "keen sympathy and anxious interest" when he has done the opposite; her tone is sarcastic. It is not her pride that's hurt, eliminating A. She feels no compassion for Orgon's senseless behavior, and certainly no affection, eliminating B and E. D is incorrect because she is not frightened in any way.

38. **ANSWER: E.** *A tone question.* Dorine's assurance that when Orgon's wife became ill, Tartuffe "bore it very well" is heavily sarcastic because Tartuffe didn't have to bear anything. She is, as Cléante says, laughing in Orgon's face with her sarcasm. Dorine's answer in A is literal and carries no irony since she is not yet laughing at Orgon. The other lines are matter-of-fact statements about Orgon's wife's health and are intended more to develop sympathy for her, not to ridicule Orgon, as E does.

39. **ANSWER: A.** *A question of interpretation.* Orgon can't finish the sentence because he doesn't have a positive example to give of Tartuffe's excellence. B is wrong because Orgon is not angry at this point. E can't be correct because there's no humility in Tartuffe to violate, and both C and D contradict the text.

40. **ANSWER: C.** *An irony question.* When Cléante tells Orgon that Dorine was laughing in his face, he meant literally that she was mocking him. All the other choices are ironic: A because Orgon should be concerned about his wife's health, not Tartuffe's; B because we would expect to meet a freeloading scrounge in many places, but not a in church; D because if Orgon has been "reborn," it is as a fool; and E because Tartuffe's interests seem to be exclusively with physical pleasure in a world he sees as anything but a dunghill—as long as someone else is paying.

41. **ANSWER: E.** *An interpretation question.* Orgon's failure to hear what he's being told about his wife makes him obnoxious, and his mechanical persistence makes him laughable. While we might feel some "pity" or "anger," choices A and D can be eliminated because no details back up the "fear" or the "despair" that must accompany them. We may be embarrassed, but the embarrassment is for Orgon, not for ourselves, and B is a weaker response than E because it fails to include the intention of humor.

42. **ANSWER: D.** *A question of comic technique.* Cléante's assumption about the country is logical and straightforward. All the others have situations upside-down. In A, Orgon should be more worried about his wife than about Tartuffe. In B, Tartuffe is behaving like the owner of the house instead of as a guest. In C, the older Orgon should be setting an example for Dorine, but it is the young woman who behaves sensibly. In E, Tartuffe's reaction to Orgon's wife's being bled should be to look out for her instead of for his own comfort.

43. **ANSWER: D.** *A rhyme scheme question—not a common type, but they still appear.* The rhyming couplets should be obvious; they are a convention of French classical theater but tend to sound odd to us. None of the other choices appears with any regularity in the passage.

44. **ANSWER: A.** *A question of intent and technique.* The satire is directed at Orgon, and the comedy in his persistent refusal to hear and understand is so broad that it approaches slapstick. B, D, and E can be eliminated because they overlook the comedy—the scene's most obvious technique. C is a less satisfying choice than A because it puts the emphasis on Tartuffe when the scene is about Orgon and because "lighthearted" misses the point of the seriousness of the satire.

45. **ANSWER: C.** *A speaker question.* The speaker identifies herself in lines 18–19, "old woman / or nearly so, myself." Choices B, D, and E name people who are mentioned but who do not speak the lines. Choice A is closer since the student who is the subject of lines 13–16 is the same person as the woman in line 18, but the speaker tells the story of the poem as an older woman, not as the student, who (the poem says) would not see the story as worth telling.

46. **ANSWER: B.** *A setting question.* In a literal sense, the setting is the museum because the speaker "thinks through" the whole piece while standing in that museum, but there is no "museum only" choice. The poem's story that makes up the speaker's thought begins in the classroom with the teacher's question. In line 17 it moves to the "real museum," where the speaker is standing for the rest of the poem. Choice D fails to see that change. The places named in A, C, and E don't exist in the poem.

47. **ANSWER: B.** *A question of diction and interpretation.* The teacher poses the question, identifying a painting by a specific artist—Rembrandt—and an old woman. When the speaker gives us the children's point of view in line 7, the specificity of the Rembrandt painting fades into the generic term "art," and the old woman is stripped of her gender and even her humanity as she becomes "old age." Choice E might at first appear defensible, but the poem doesn't give us the teacher's reaction, so we don't know if he or she in fact feels frustration.

48. ANSWER: **A**. *An interpretation question.* The speaker as a child cannot picture an "old woman," since she thinks only in terms of "old age." In order to get a specific image in her mind, she turns to the only "old" woman she can think of, her grandmother (who probably has much longer to live than the "old woman" the teacher has in mind). The speaker then uses "borrow" as a metaphor for her own moving of the face from one woman to another. Choices B and C specify emotions not present in the poem, E strays from the text because there's no mention of lighting, and D is wrong because the teacher doesn't mention grandparents.

49. ANSWER: **B**. *A diction and tone question.* The teacher chooses the overly formal word "eschews" instead of the more natural "avoids" or more conversational "is trying to get out of" that the children would understand more easily. The teacher is rebuking Linda, but the scolding is indirect and fairly gentle. Choices A and E far overstate the tone of the teacher's remark. Choice D is correct in identifying the aloof tone, but if the teacher were either untroubled or indifferent, there would have been no rebuke at all. The word "nostalgia" eliminates C.

50. ANSWER: **E**. *A reference question.* The old woman is the speaker, as is made clear by the surrounding pronouns "I" in line 17 and "myself" in line 19. A is wrong because we are not told the subject of the Rembrandt painting, and C and D are incorrect because the people named don't appear in the poem. B can't be right because we don't know the teacher's age or gender.

51. ANSWER: **A**. *A symbol question.* The seasons often symbolize a human life from the youth of spring, maturing of summer, aging of autumn, and death of winter. That's the case here. Nothing about the children would link them to autumn, eliminating A. Choices C, D, and E have nothing in the poem to defend choosing them.

52. ANSWER: **C**. *A structure question.* Every poem will have at least one shift. Here the two parts are each introduced by the announcement of a place and time. Line 1 gives us "[I]n . . . class so many years ago," and line 17, "[t]his fall in a real museum." That change in setting marks the poem's move from a more narrative section to a more reflective one. Choice E could be defended as the place where the poem turns from all past observations to a concluding sentence, but it lacks the structural reinforcement of the abrupt setting change at line 17. Choice D is harder to support because although the poem moves into metaphor there, it moves back in the next sentence. Choices A and B have little to suggest a major shift.

53. ANSWER: **E**. *A tone question.* The reflective nature of the whole poem results in the realistic conclusion that the children cannot yet understand enough to make the decision the teacher has asked for. Choice A is inaccurate because only half the poem is set in the past, and the look back carries no nostalgia. There is no whimsy to justify choice B, and while the speaker may be disappointed that the children cannot understand, there is nothing pessimistic or "mournful" in her realization, so C and D are wrong.

54. **ANSWER: C.** *A speaker question.* The speaker here identifies with the teacher's "old woman," even calling herself "old woman" in line 18. We are not told what is in the Rembrandt, eliminating B. Choice A is wrong because the speaker doesn't identify with the teacher. The speaker understands that the question the teacher poses has little meaning to the children; there is no evidence that the teacher does. Although she sympathizes to some extent with the children on their "hard chairs," she is far from feeling herself one of them, eliminating D. Only choice E offers some temptation, but the speaker puts the grandmother in an "imagined museum" and contrasts it explicitly with the "real museum" she is in.

55. **ANSWER: D.** *A question about the main idea—a most common type.* All the choices have support in the poem except the idea that the children are "closer to 'the browns of earth.'" In fact, the speaker unequivocally includes "season" in the list of things "beyond saving by children." The hard chairs distract children from their task, ruling out A. Linda and, we can safely assume, the other children would rather skip the question than answer it, so B is out. Choice C can't be the exception because the children are inconsistent in their choices, and E is wrong, because it nearly paraphrases the poem's conclusion.

SCORING GUIDELINES FOR SECTION II

The score reported for each essay reflects the reader's judgment of the quality of the essay as a whole. Readers are instructed to reward the writers for what they do well. The score for an exceptionally well-written essay may be raised by one point. A poorly written essay can be scored no higher than a 3.

SCORING GUIDELINES FOR QUESTION 1

9–8 These detailed, well-written essays provide insightful analysis of Glück's poem. They marshal apt and specific details from the poem to lead compellingly to well-founded conclusions. They acknowledge that "happily ever after" does not operate here, and they give some sort of expression to the idea that this Gretel can be seen to represent more people than the girl in the fairy tale. They elaborate effectively on the "darkness" in the title and relate it to the darkness in the poem. They select significant techniques and illustrate their impact on a meaning of the poem, one the essay states or implies clearly. These essays may propose a range of readings and explain a variety of techniques. They may not be flawless, but they sustain their control over the elements of effective writing and manage some measure of style.

7–6 These competent essays offer a consistent understanding of the poem, including both its darkness for Gretel and its divergence from the standard fairy tale ending. They deal specifically with the title, although possibly less thoroughly than the top essays. Their interpretations may weaken in some particulars or exaggerate or exploit an idea beyond its worth, or they may be less detailed or precise. They link their discussion to an expressed meaning of the poem but may do so less convincingly. While they may not demonstrate the same control or sophistication as the 9–8 essays, they do provide evidence of an ability to express logical ideas with clarity and some control.

5 These essays demonstrate some understanding of Gretel's attitude, but they may tend to be more superficial and less compelling than the upper-half essays. They recognize the darkness but may relate it only in part or to a meaning of the poem as a whole. Their argument may slight part of the prompt or rest on insufficient support from concrete detail in the text. They may present minor misreading but show an understanding of the poem's central ideas. There may be some paraphrase, but there are attempts to use it in analysis. The writing shows some control, although maybe not a comfortable command. Mechanical errors are not so distracting as to force rereading, and the diction is not so bland or vague as to obscure meaning. They may not be as well planned or developed as those scoring higher, but they are adequate.

4–3 These lower-half essays reveal an incomplete understanding of the poem, the task, or both. They may suffer more serious misreading or slight their discussion of the poem in favor of the fairy tale. They may fail to recognize the poetic techniques at work in the poem, or they may simply name them without attempting to link them to their intended effect on a reader. They may present interpretations that are not supported by the detail in the poem or that misrepresent or seriously exaggerate what should be minor concerns. The writing may ramble or veer away from the task, or it may fall into extended paraphrase without links to meaning. These essays show an ability to express basic ideas but demonstrate uncertain control over writing beyond the sentence level. Essays that include significant misreading or unskilled writing should be scored 3.

2–1 These essays compound the weaknesses of the 4–3 essays. They may be unacceptably brief or may badly misread the poem. Although they make some attempt to respond to the task, they do so without clarity, organization, or supporting example. They may be poorly written on several counts and include distracting errors in grammar and mechanics that frequently force rereading. Essays with little coherent discussion of the poem should be scored 1.

0 These essays may make no more than a reference to the task.

— These essays are either left blank or are completely off topic.

Scoring Guidelines for Question 2

9–8 These well-constructed essays demonstrate a grasp of the complexity of this seemingly simple tale. They identify, usually explicitly, more than one meaning and link the meanings to the story's title. They will draw on a range of symbolic interpretations but keep them well grounded in the text. Building on apt references to Updike's text, these essays offer a compelling explanation of the literary techniques (such as detail, diction, or syntax) that Updike uses to create and convey meaning. While they may not be without flaws, these papers attest to an ability to sustain control over the elements of effective writing and manage some measure of style and confidence.

7–6 These competent essays offer a consistent understanding of the story and of ways in which some of its multiple meanings relate to the title. They may not be as responsive to the complexities of the story as the top essays, but they provide apt and specific references to the text. Their analysis may be less persuasive or may exaggerate or exploit a simple idea beyond its worth, and their evidence may be thinner than the 9–8 papers. Although they may lack the fullness and the rich specificity of the top essays, may explain fewer techniques, and may have less detail than the top essays, they do provide evidence of an ability to read with some insight and to express logical ideas with clarity and some control.

5 These essays offer a reasonable although often reductive reading of Updike's story. Their discussion of meaning may be more superficial and predictable and may be expressed in more pedestrian language. They may slight the title with a simple mention and may fall into plot summary, although with attempts to link that summary to analysis. The organization may be unsuccessful or incomplete. There may be slight misinterpretations or exaggerations of particular references or the discussion of some may be not fully realized. The writing shows some control, although not a comfortable command. It is not marked by persistently distracting mechanical errors that force rereading or by diction so bland or vague as to obscure meaning. They may not be as well planned or developed as those scoring higher, but they are adequate.

4–3 These lower-half essays reveal an incomplete understanding of the story, the task, or both. Typically they are unable to go beyond the simple surface of the story. They may fail to recognize the literary techniques at work in the story, or they may simply name them without attempting to link them to their intended effect on meaning. They may present interpretations that are not supported by the text or that misrepresent or seriously exaggerate what should be minor concerns. The writing may ramble or veer away from the task, or it may fall into extended plot summary without links to meaning. These essays show an ability to express basic ideas but demonstrate uncertain control over writing beyond the sentence level. Essays that include significant misreading or unskilled writing should be scored 3.

2–1 These essays compound the weaknesses of the 4–3 essays. They may be unacceptably brief or may badly misinterpret the story. Although they attempt to respond to the task, they do so without clarity, organization, or supporting example. They may be poorly written on several counts and include distracting errors in grammar and mechanics that force rereading. Essays with little coherent discussion of the story should be scored 1.

0 These essays may make no more than a reference to the task.

— These essays are either left blank or are completely off topic.

Scoring Guidelines for Question 3

9–8 These persuasive essays identify a character in an appropriate novel, play, or epic who takes on another identity or nature. They explain with precision and rich concrete detail from the text the differences between the character's true nature and the feigned identity. They articulate clearly a meaning of the work as a whole and show compellingly how the role they have defined relates to the character's adopted identity. While the change in identity may not be central to the literary work, it is to these essays. They are not without flaw, but they are focused and organized, and alternate with skill between the details of the text and the writer's comment on that detail. They show that the student reads with perception and has a practiced and sophisticated control over the techniques of expressing that perception.

7–6 These essays present a rational and credible explanation of the impact on a clearly stated meaning of the work by the character's pretending. The account of that relationship may be more mechanical or less smoothly articulated, and the essays less thorough or specific than the top papers, but they demonstrate both an accurate reading of the work and sufficient control over the elements of writing about literature. Essays scored 7 will have stronger textual support for their claims and, generally, more expertise of expression than those scored 6.

5 These acceptable essays may be superficial in their expression of the relationship of the changed identity to a meaning of the work. They may confuse pretending with delusion, in which the character may not have chosen the new role. They may overexplain the obvious or belabor predictable ideas rather than offer insight. Plot summary may play too large a role, but plot summary is still linked to an attempt at analysis. While the writing may be inexact in diction and lack grace in syntax, it is still adequate to the expression of the writer's ideas.

4–3 These lower-half essays are incomplete in their understanding of either the prompt or the works they purport to analyze, or both. They may choose a character's pretense that they cannot successfully relate to a meaning of the work or they may be unable to articulate such a meaning clearly. They may fail to go beyond restating what is evident in a plot line or be carried away by plot summary. The writing may fail to show organization and control over the content and the form. This is the highest score for an essay that avoids identifying a meaning of the work as a whole or whose organizational or mechanical weakness forces continuous rereading and backtracking.

2–1 These essays compound the weaknesses of the 3–4 papers. They may completely misconstrue the actual purpose of an author's changing a character's identity or nature or may pay little heed to the instructions. Typically they are unacceptable in form, in content, or both. While they address the prompt, they do so in a cursory, fleeting, or ineffective way. Essays scored 2 include some analysis, however rudimentary. Essays scored 1 include no worthwhile comment on the work.

0 These essays may refer to the prompt but make no attempt to respond to it.

— These essays are blank or write completely off the task.

come from washing dishes in a dishpan with a rag-plugged hole on an oilcloth-covered table by light of a coal-oil lamp. I kept everything shining.

The bathroom too. I had a bath in there once a week. They wouldn't have minded if I took one oftener, but to me it seemed like asking too 10 much, or maybe risking making it less wonderful. The basin and the tub and the toilet were all pink, and there were glass doors with flamingos painted on them, to shut off the tub. The light had a rose cast and the mat sank under your feet like snow, except that it was warm. The mirror was three-way. With the mirror all steamed up and the air 15 like a perfume cloud, from things I was allowed to use, I stood up on the side of the tub and admired myself naked, from three directions. Sometimes I thought about the way we lived out at home and the way we lived here and how one way was so hard to imagine when you were living the other way. But I thought it was still a lot easier, living the way 20 we lived at home, to picture something like this, the painted flamingos and the warmth and the soft mat, than it was anybody knowing only things like this to picture how it was the other way. And why was that?

I was through my jobs in no time, and had the vegetables peeled for supper and sitting in cold water besides. Then I went into Mrs. 25 Peebles' bedroom. I had been in there plenty of times, cleaning, and I always took a good look in her closet, at the clothes she had hanging there. I wouldn't have looked in her drawers, but a closet is open to anybody. That's a lie. I would have looked in drawers, but I would have felt worse doing it and been more scared she could tell. 30

Some clothes in her closet she wore all the time, I was quite familiar with them. Others she never put on, they were pushed to the back. I was disappointed to see no wedding dress. But there was one long dress I could just see the skirt of, and I was hungering to see the rest. Now I took note of where it hung and lifted it out. It was satin, a lovely 35 weight on my arm, light bluish-green in color, almost silvery. It had a fitted, pointed waist and a full skirt and an off-the-shoulder fold hiding the little sleeves.

Next thing was easy. I got out of my own things and slipped it on. I was slimmer at fifteen than anybody would believe who knows me now 40 and the fit was beautiful. I didn't, of course, have a strapless bra on, which was what it needed, I just had to slide my straps down my arms under the material. Then I tried pinning up my hair, to get the effect. One thing led to another. I put on rouge and lipstick and eyebrow pencil from her dresser. The heat of the day and the weight of the satin 45 and all the excitement made me thirsty, and I went out to the kitchen, got-up as I was, to get a glass of ginger ale with ice cubes from the refrigerator. The Peebleses drank ginger ale, or fruit drinks, all day, like water, and I was getting so I did too. Also there was no limit on ice cubes, which I was so fond of I would even put them in a glass of milk. 50

GO ON TO THE NEXT PAGE

34. The passage is primarily concerned with
    (A) presenting a description of the Pebbleses' home
    (B) denigrating Edie's fitness for her job
    (C) exposing the inequalities of class and economics
    (D) establishing Edie's character
    (E) justifying the invasion of personal privacy

35. The primary functions of the opening paragraph include all of the following EXCEPT to
    (A) establish that the story is being told as a flashback
    (B) imply the young woman's pride in the quality of her work
    (C) establish the difference between the young woman's family's home and the house where she lives in the passage
    (D) set the plot in motion
    (E) begin the detailed description that will continue throughout the passage

36. From the details in the first thirteen lines, we can infer that the home the speaker came from had
    (A) electric lights
    (B) an enclosed bath or shower
    (C) a kitchen sink
    (D) running water
    (E) a clean kitchen

37. The phrase "risking making it less wonderful" (line 11) implies that
    (A) Edie has come to see her new home as normal
    (B) Edie sees the weekly bath as a special event
    (C) the Peebleses would disapprove of Edie's using the bath more often
    (D) Edie's using the bath often would jeopardize it for others
    (E) the bath is not the wonderful experience Edit had hoped

38. The narrator implies that Edie sees the situation in which she finds herself as a kind of
    (A) lasting nightmare
    (B) irreversible profligacy
    (C) unproductive fantasy
    (D) pleasant luxury
    (E) dispiriting futility

39. Lines 20–23 differ from the rest of the passage in that they
    (A) contrast two ways of life
    (B) offer specific and concrete descriptions
    (C) present a brief meditation on an abstraction
    (D) allow the narrator to reveal her thoughts
    (E) accent the distance between the narrator and the younger woman she was

40. The humor in the phrase "no limit on ice cubes" (lines 49–50) results from all of the following EXCEPT
    (A) the discrepancy between Edie's concept of extravagance and the actual cost of the ice cubes
    (B) Edie's concern about a limit on a family item like ice when she's wearing private items like another's makeup and clothes
    (C) the curious picture of Edie using ice cubes in her glass of milk
    (D) Edie's home having no ice cubes at all
    (E) the contrast of the idea of a limit on ice cubes with Edie's notion of herself in the borrowed dress

41. The passage as a whole is developed chiefly through
    (A) metaphor and simile
    (B) description and narration
    (C) analysis and definition
    (D) comparison and contrast
    (E) proposition and counterargument

42. Based on the passage as a whole, the young woman is best characterized as
    (A) insightful and creative
    (B) experienced and polished
    (C) adventuresome and courageous
    (D) reticent and inhibited
    (E) naïve and sincere

43. The passage as a whole employs all of the following contrasts EXCEPT one between
    (A) the Edie in the passage and the Edie who narrates it
    (B) comfort and privation
    (C) Edie's past and her situation in the passage
    (D) Edie's circumstances in the passage and her hopes
    (E) Edie's clothes and Mrs. Peebles's clothes

44. The tone of the passage as a whole is best characterized as
    (A) fatalistic and accepting
    (B) insincere and frantic
    (C) lethargic and indifferent
    (D) genuine and unguarded
    (E) playful and jovial

QUESTIONS 45–55. Carefully read the poem by Richard Wilbur before choosing your answers.

The Writer

In her room at the prow of the house
Where light breaks, and the windows are tossed with linden,
My daughter is writing a story.

I pause in the stairwell, hearing
From her shut door a commotion of typewriter-keys   5
Like a chain hauled over a gunwale.

Young as she is, the stuff
Of her life is a great cargo, and some of it heavy:
I wish her a lucky passage.

But now it is she who pauses,   10
As if to reject my thought and its easy figure.
A stillness greatens, in which

The whole house seems to be thinking,
And then she is at it again with a bunched clamor
Of strokes, and again is silent.   15

I remember the dazed starling
Which was trapped in that very room, two years ago;
How we stole in, lifted a sash

And retreated, not to affright it;
And how for a helpless hour, through the crack of the door, 20
We watched the sleek, wild, dark

And iridescent creature
Batter against the brilliance, drop like a glove
To the hard floor, or the desk-top,

And wait then, humped and bloody,   25
For the wits to try it again; and how our spirits
Rose when, suddenly sure,

Question 2

Carefully read the short story by Lan Samantha Chang, printed here in its entirety. Then write an essay in which you show how the writer reveals the meaning of the story through the interplay of the contemporary setting and action with the ancient legend. In your essay you might want to consider such elements as title, detail, and symbol.

Water Names

Summertime at dusk we'd gather on the back porch, tired and sticky from another day of fierce encoded quarrels, nursing our mosquito bites and frail dignities, sisters in name only. At first we'd pinch and slap each other, fighting for the best—least ragged—folding chair. Then we'd argue over who would sit next to our 5
grandmother. We were so close together on the tiny porch that we often pulled our own hair by mistake. Forbidden to bite, we planted silent toothmarks on each other's wrists. We ignored the bulk of house behind us, the yard, the fields, the darkening sky. We even forgot about our grandmother. Then suddenly we'd hear her old, 10
dry voice, very close, almost on the backs of our necks.

"*Xiushila!* Shame on you. Fighting like a bunch of chickens."

And Ingrid, the oldest, would freeze with her thumb and forefinger right on the back of Lily's arm. I would slide my hand away from the end of Ingrid's braid. Ashamed, we would shuffle 15
our feet while Waipuo calmly found her chair.

On some nights she sat with us in silence, the tip of her cigarette glowing red like a distant stoplight. But on some nights she told us stories, "just to keep up your Chinese," she said, and the red dot flickered and danced, making ghostly shapes as she moved 20
her hands like a magician in the dark.

"In these prairie crickets I often hear the sound of rippling waters, of the Yangtze River," she said. "Granddaughters, you are descended on both sides from people of the water country, near the mouth of the great Chang Jiang, as it is called, where the river is so 25
grand and broad that even on clear days you can scarcely see the other side.

"The Chang Jiang runs four thousand miles, originating in the Himalaya mountains where it crashes, flecked with gold dust, down steep cliffs so perilous and remote that few humans have ever seen 30
them. In central China, the river squeezes through deep gorges, then widens in its last thousand miles to the sea. Our ancestors have lived near the mouth of this river, the ever-changing delta, near a city called Nanjing, for more than a thousand years."

"A thousand years," murmured Lily, who was only ten. When 35
she was younger she had sometimes burst into nervous crying at the thought of so many years. Her small insistent fingers grabbed my fingers in the dark.

"Through your mother and I you are descended from a line of great men and women. We have survived countless floods and 40
seasons of ill-fortune because we have the spirit of the river in us. Unlike mountains, we cannot be powdered down or broken apart. Instead, we run together, like raindrops. Our strength and spirit wear down mountains into sand. But even our people must respect the water." 45

She paused, and a bit of ash glowed briefly as it drifted to the floor.

"When I was young, my own grandmother once told me the story of Wen Zhiqing's daughter. Twelve hundred years ago the civilized part of China still lay to the north, and the Yangtze valley 50 lay unspoiled. In those days lived an ancestor named Wen Zhiqing, a resourceful man, and proud. He had been fishing for many years with trained cormorants, which you girls of course have never seen. Cormorants are sleek, black birds with long, bending necks which the fishermen fitted with metal rings so the fish they caught could 55 not be swallowed. The birds would perch on the side of the old wooden boat and dive into the river." We had only known blue swimming pools, but we tried to imagine the sudden shock of cold and the plunge, deep into water.

"Now, Wen Zhiqing had a favorite daughter who was very 60 beautiful and loved the river. She would beg to go out on the boat with him. This daughter was a restless one, never contented with their catch, and often she insisted they stay out until it was almost dark. Even then, she was not satisfied. She had been spoiled by her father, kept protected from the river, so she could not see its 65 danger. To this young woman, the river was as familiar as the sky. It was a bright, broad road stretching out to curious lands. She did not fully understand the river's depths.

"One clear spring evening, as she watched the last bird dive off into the blackening waters, she said, 'If only this catch would bring 70 back something more than another fish!'

"She leaned over the side of the boat and looked at the water. The stars and moon reflected back at her. And it is said that the spirits living underneath the water looked up at her as well. And the spirit of a young man who had drowned in the river many years 75 before saw her lovely face."

We had heard about the ghosts of the drowned, who wait forever in the water for a living person to pull down instead. A faint breeze moved through the mosquito screens and we shivered.

"The cormorant was gone for a very long time," Waipuo said, 80 "so long that the fishermen grew puzzled. Then, suddenly, the bird emerged from the waters, almost invisible in the night. Wen Zhiqing grasped his catch, a very large fish, and guided the boat back to shore. And when Wen reached home, he gutted the fish and discovered, in its stomach, a valuable pearl ring." 85

"From the man?" said Lily.

"Sshh, she'll tell you."

Waipuo ignored us. "His daughter was delighted that her wish had been fulfilled. What most excited her was the idea of an entire world like this, a world where such a beautiful ring would be only a 90 bauble. For part of her had always longed to see faraway things and places. The river had put a spell on her heart. In the evenings she began to sit on the bank, looking at her own reflection in the water. Sometimes she said she saw a handsome young man looking back at her. And her yearning for him filled her heart with sorrow 95 and fear, for she knew that she would soon leave her beloved family.

"'It's just the moon,' said Wen Zhiqing, but his daughter shook her head. 'There's a kingdom under the water,' she said. 'The prince

GO ON TO THE NEXT PAGE

ANSWERS AND EXPLANATIONS FOR SECTION I

MULTIPLE-CHOICE ANSWER KEY

Using the table below, determine how many questions you answered correctly, how many incorrectly. Then look over the answer explanations.

1. B	2. D	3. E	4. D	5. B
6. D	7. D	8. A	9. D	10. B
11. D	12. C	13. C	14. B	15. B
16. E	17. D	18. A	19. A	20. E
21. D	22. E	23. A	24. D	25. E
26. C	27. D	28. A	29. C	30. D
31. D	32. C	33. C	34. D	35. D
36. E	37. B	38. D	39. C	40. D
41. B	42. E	43. A	44. D	45. C
46. E	47. B	48. B	49. E	50. A
51. A	52. D	53. B	54. E	55. B

EXPLANATIONS FOR THE MULTIPLE-CHOICE ANSWERS

1. **ANSWER: B.** *An interpretation question.* The tasks are all either physically impossible or hopeless because they depend on myth and legend, like the shape of the Devil's foot or the singing mermaids. Only the reference to the Devil has a religious connotation, eliminating A and D. The "envy" might relate to love (C), but the others could do so only metaphorically. Because they're all impossible, none would relate to line 20.

2. **ANSWER: D.** *A rhyme question.* Multi-syllable rhymes are nearly always intended to bring a smile. The "singing / stinging" rhyme of lines 5–6 begins to suggest humor; the humor in the rhyme of "tell me / befell thee" in lines 14–15 is even stronger, and the almost silly "met her/letter" (lines 23–24) makes the humorous intent inescapable. A careful reading reveals that the words involved have no special importance, eliminating A. B doesn't work because the three sets are not related in any way. The lines don't continue the *abab* rhyme that precedes them, but break it, eliminating C, and E has to be a distractor because the rhythm is neither steady nor broken by the rhyme.

3. ANSWER: E. *An interpretation question.* The star, the root, and the wind are from the natural world, the Devil is a religious figure; mermaids come to us from mythology; and envy is a psychological emotion. None on the list, though, relate directly to health.

4. ANSWER: D. *An interpretation/vocabulary question.* The meaning of the line depends on the word "born," used here in the sense of "destined from birth." A, B, and C all build on a different definition of being born, and E offers a choice based on another word entirely, the verb "to bear," meaning "to carry or support."

5. ANSWER: B. *A grammar question.* The verb "to snow" is normally intransitive. Here, it's used in its transitive sense of "to cause to fall like snow." The image is of the white hair descending to cover the head as the person ages.

6. ANSWER: D. *A vocabulary and implication question.* The lines say that a woman both "true" (faithful) and "fair" (beautiful) lives "no where." The distractors all play on a misreading of the two adjectives describing the woman.

7. ANSWER: D. *A grammar question.* In these questions the pronoun rarely refers to the most recent noun. Here, though, it does. The second stanza establishes that the search is for "a woman true, and fair." The speaker here asks to be told if "one," meaning such a woman, is found.

8. ANSWER: A. *A grammar question.* "Me" refers to the speaker; the "who" in the next line refers to whatever power gave the Devil feet like a goat, presumably God, but certainly not the speaker. Both the choices in B refer to the speaker, those in D refer to the person addressed, and those in C and E refer to the theoretical woman.

9. ANSWER: D. *An interpretation question.* The opening words of line 21 make it clear that the speaker is giving up the hunt even before it begins. The rest of the stanza only adds "even though" phrases to reinforce his abandoning the search. All the others imply or state that the speaker wants to keep looking.

10. ANSWER: B. *A figurative language question.* Riding for ten thousand days works out to over 27 years on the horse; that qualifies easily as hyperbole, or extravagant exaggeration.

11. ANSWER: D. *A thematic question.* The idea that the speaker could not in a lifetime find one woman to fit the search is so exaggerated that we know he's not entirely serious. He sounds unhappy, and we can make some guesses about why. That unhappiness eliminates B, C, and E, and because God doesn't figure in the poem, A is wrong.

12. ANSWER: C. *An interpretation question.* Immediately after calling himself naïve, the speaker speaks of the questions "which I, and only I, could answer." He will come to understand that others cannot tell him who he is.

13. **ANSWER: C.** *An interpretation question.* It is the white community that doesn't see the narrator as an individual. A, D, and E can be eliminated because of the declaration that the graduation oration was "a triumph for our whole community," and that would include his parents and the audience. The grandfather singles him out for his deathbed advice, eliminating B.

14. **ANSWER: B.** *An interpretation question.* The narrator maintains that he is a distinct individual but that his grandparents' being enslaved and then freed but still unequal is the history that makes him who he is. A, C, and D have to be wrong because they contradict the text. He is, as he says, what history has made him, regardless of any advice he may have received.

15. **ANSWER: B.** *An interpretation question.* The phrase means inevitable, so he means his future had been decided. D and E misunderstand the word "cards." A contradicts the text, and, contrary to predicting anything for him, his grandfather gives him advice.

16. **ANSWER: E.** *A question of reference.* The reference is to unequal civil rights. The image of the hand with separate fingers that work together hints at the concept that races in America could be given "separate but equal" facilities and rights. So the fingers here are a symbol of inequalities of opportunity. The other choices refer to the text, but inappropriately.

17. **ANSWER: D.** *A question of chronology and interpretation.* Since D refers to the grandfather's behavior before he made the statement, it cannot "result" from it. All the others list the changing stages of the narrator's realization of different meanings of the advice.

18. **ANSWER: A.** *A contrast question.* We see no major difference between the grandfather and the narrator, who, in fact, says he carried out the old man's advice. The differences between the two elements in each of the other choices are explicitly named in the text. He says the answers of others were "often in contradiction" (lines 3–4), eliminating B. He says he was "asking everyone," but realized they were questions "only I could answer" (lines 5–6), and that he "accepted their answers" (line 3) but that "I am nobody but myself" (line 8), eliminating C. The grandfather had been "the meekest of men" (line 28), in contrast to his deathbed words, eliminating D. Finally, E can't be the answer because the narrator says that "the white folks, . . . if they had understood they would have desired me to act just the opposite" (lines 49–50).

19. **ANSWER: A.** *A grammar question.* The grandfather identifies "'em" in line 23 as "the enemy." Since he has had no conflict with the family, E can be ruled out. The grandfather never speaks of undermining principles of any kind, eliminating B and C. D won't work because the image of the hand is the narrator's, not the grandfather's.

20. **ANSWER: E.** *A structure question.* Although it is principally expository, the passage narrates the grandfather's advice and mentions other events, such as the graduation oration. The other choices name rhetorical patterns that the narrator does not use here.

21. ANSWER: D. *A grammar question.* The narrator admits to feeling guilty about carrying out his grandfather's advice, even more because others approved of his behavior. The "constant puzzle" is private to the narrator and, as such, could not bring approval, eliminating B. C contradicts the text because the narrator says he carries the advice constantly. The text doesn't support E because we see no interaction between the narrator and the "younguns."

22. ANSWER: E. *A question of purpose.* The narrator states his task clearly in the opening paragraph and then goes on to develop it. Although he questions his grandfather's advice, he follows it, eliminating A. The oration needs no justification since everyone praises it, eliminating B. How valid the grandfather's advice is we don't learn in the passage; we know only that the narrator questions it throughout, eliminating C. The expressed disapproval of the white men is brief and too general to serve as a main purpose.

23. ANSWER: A. *A question of similarities.* The two lines establish the child's idyllic relationship with the farm, with the wagons honoring him. In line 10 the relationship is reinforced, and the child is now "famous among the barns." B, C, and D fail to work because none of them mention the child at all. E does but the child is now in chains, so the meaning has shifted.

24. ANSWER: D. *An allusion question.* The line turns the conventional fairytale opening of "once upon a time" to the playful "once below a time." The word "lord" might appear at first to suggest medieval or mythological stories, but nothing further supports the idea, eliminating A and B. C has no basis in either the poem or Greek myth, and there is no link to the house in line 2, so E is wrong.

25. ANSWER: E. *An interpretation question.* As the child lies in that halfway place between waking and sleep, he hears owls outside and associates the sound with slipping into dreams. Nothing in the poem suggests any harmful or frightful aspects of owls, eliminating the other choices.

26. ANSWER: C. *An allusion question.* A mention of the "story of Adam and Eve" suggests the serpent and the coming of sin. The speaker here wants the Garden of Eden image, but while it is still "shining" and pure. To keep that purity, the speaker substitutes "maiden" for Eve's name. The child's ignorance of the story is irrelevant to the poem, eliminating A. B is contrary to the speaker's intention, and D and E have no support in the text.

27. ANSWER: D. *An allusion question.* The allusion is to the child's state of grace, or innocence, a state that lines 44–45 suggest time will one day end. A, B, and C build on other meanings of the word "grace," meanings not intended here. E has no basis in the text; the "natural country way of life" would probably not be consistent with the innocence intended here.

28. ANSWER: A. *A figurative language question.* The speaker personifies time beginning in lines 4, 13, 42, 46, and 53. None of the others are named explicitly in the poem.

52. **ANSWER: D.** *An interpretation question.* The narrator has learned what the daughter is learning—the writing, while the writer is doing it, becomes a matter "of life and death," one of awe-inspiring significance. A and B try to impose meanings that the poem doesn't address. There are dangers in adolescence, but the speaker doesn't address them, and we don't know that the daughter is an adolescent. Choice C misreads the word "death" as referring to the speaker's own literal death when the word is used here figuratively. E can be eliminated because the daughter doesn't even know about the image; the speaker only imagines her rejecting it ("as if to reject . . .").

53. **ANSWER: B.** *An interpretation question.* The last stanza doesn't differentiate the two parts of the poem, it unites them by bringing together the daughter's attempts—noisy and thoughtful—to write her story with the "life or death" attempts of the starling to "clear . . . the sill of the world." The last three lines accomplish all the others.

54. **ANSWER: E.** *An implication question.* Like looking in a mirror that reflects a mirror facing it, we come to see that the speaker is struggling to write about his daughter's struggling to write. A is wrong because the last stanza reinforces the meaning of the first 15 lines, in which the speaker wishes the daughter "a lucky passage." We know nothing about previous poems, eliminating B. C fails to understand that lines 31–32 say she has no choice—and that there's nothing more serious than "life and death." D is wrong because the speaker has intentionally rejected the original metaphor of the ship.

55. **ANSWER: B.** *A tone question.* The speaker meditates on both his daughter's writing and the starling's predicament. He shows affection for both by wishing—twice—for his daughter and by taking care "not to affright" the bird and having his spirit "soar" when it flies free. C, D, and E all infer negative connotations that the poem does not imply. A comes closer but oversimplifies the complexity of the poem. There is little that is "playful" about it except the play with language, and "serious" connotes a solemnity that isn't there.

SCORING GUIDELINES FOR SECTION II

The score reported for each essay reflects the reader's judgment of the quality of the essay as a whole. Readers are instructed to reward the writers for what they do well. The score for an exceptionally well-written essay may be raised by one point. A poorly written essay can be scored no higher than a 3.

SCORING GUIDELINES FOR QUESTION 1

9–8 These detailed, well-written essays provide an insightful analysis of Reed's poem. They marshal from the poem apt and specific details that lead compellingly to well-founded conclusions. They identify the two voices, although some will read them as two or more separate people, others as two voices from one individual whose attention shifts from the classroom or drill setting to the gardens. They elaborate effectively on contrasts in the poem and on techniques the poet uses to both link and differentiate the two settings and voices. They select significant techniques and illustrate their impact on a "purpose" the poet achieves, one the essay states or implies clearly. These essays may propose a range of readings and explain a variety of techniques. Although they may not be flawless, these papers sustain their control over the elements of effective writing and manage some measure of style.

7–6 These competent essays offer a consistent understanding of the poem, including the two settings and the shifting of the voice. They deal specifically with techniques the poet uses both to differentiate the two settings and voices, although possibly less thoroughly than the top essays. Their interpretations may weaken in some particulars or exaggerate or exploit an idea beyond its worth, or they may be less detailed or precise. They link their discussion to an expressed meaning of the poem but may settle for a less complex "purpose" than the best papers and may do so less convincingly. While they may not demonstrate the same control or sophistication as the 9–8 essays, they do provide evidence of an ability to express logical ideas with clarity and some control.

5 These essays demonstrate some understanding of the two voices but may tend to be more superficial and less compelling than the upper-half essays in exploiting their relationships. Their argument may slight one of the voices or rely on insufficient support from concrete detail in the text. They may present minor misreading but show an understanding of the poem's central purpose. There may be some paraphrase, but there are attempts to use it in analysis. The writing shows some control, although maybe not a comfortable command. Mechanical errors are not so distracting as to force rereading, and the diction is not so bland or vague as to obscure meaning. These essays may not be as well planned or developed as those scoring higher, but they are adequate.

4–3 These lower-half essays reveal an incomplete understanding of the poem, the task, or both. They may show more serious misreading, confusing or conflating the two voices, or may show the student didn't understand the task being performed through the activity of "naming the parts," or may show a misreading that suggests the assembled parts produce a rifle. They may fail to link the poet's purpose to war and peace. They sometimes fail to recognize the poetic techniques at work in the poem, or they may simply name them without attempting to link them to their intended purpose. They may present interpretations that are unsupported by the detail in the poem or that misrepresent or seriously exaggerate what should be minor concerns. The writing may ramble or veer away from the task, or it may fall into extended paraphrase without links to meaning. These essays show an ability to express basic ideas but demonstrate uncertain control over writing beyond the sentence level. Essays that include significant misreading or unskilled writing should be scored 3.

2–1 These essays compound the weaknesses of the 4–3 essays. They may be unacceptably brief or may badly misread the poem. Although they make some attempt to respond to the task, they do so without clarity, organization, or supporting example. They may be poorly written on several counts and include distracting errors in grammar and mechanics that frequently force rereading. Essays with little coherent discussion of the poem should be scored 1.

0 These essays may do no more than make reference to the task.

— These essays are either left blank or are completely off topic.

Scoring Guidelines for Question 2

9–8 These well-constructed essays demonstrate a grasp of the complexity of the relationship between the modern setting of the story and the ancient tale the grandmother tells. They identify, usually explicitly, more than one meaning and link the meanings to the story's title. They may comment perceptively on the differences in the behaviors of the girls in the first three paragraphs and in the last three. They will draw on a range of symbolic interpretations but keep them well grounded in the text. Building on apt references to Chang's text, these essays offer a compelling explanation of the literary techniques (such as detail, symbol, or diction) that create and convey meaning. While they may not be without flaws, these papers attest to an ability to sustain control over the elements of effective writing and manage some measure of style and confidence.

7–6 These competent essays offer a consistent understanding of the story and of ways in which its two parts are related. They will link the story's title to meaning, although possibly with less insight than the best essays. They may not be as responsive to the complexities of the story as the top papers, but they provide apt and specific references to the text. Their analysis may be less persuasive or may exaggerate or exploit a simple idea beyond its worth, and their evidence may be thinner than the 9–8 essays. Although they may lack the fullness and the rich specificity of the top essays, may explain fewer elements, and may have less detail than the top essays, they do provide evidence of an ability to read with some insight and to express logical ideas with clarity and some control.

5 These essays offer a reasonable although often reductive reading of Chang's story. Their attempts to link the two parts of the story and their discussion of meaning may be more superficial and predictable and may be expressed in more pedestrian language. They may slight the title with a simple mention and may fall into plot summary, although with attempts to link that summary to analysis. The organization may be unsuccessful or incomplete. There may be slight misinterpretations or exaggerations. The control of the tools of effective communication will be sufficient. Mechanical errors, though often present, are not serious or prevalent enough to force rereading. These essays are not as well organized or developed as those scoring higher, but they are adequate.

4–3 These lower-half essays reveal an incomplete understanding of the story, the task, or both. Typically they are unable to go beyond the simple surface of the story and fail to see any links between the two parts. They may fail to recognize the literary elements at work in the story, or they may simply name them without attempting to link them to their intended effect on meaning. They may present interpretations that are unsupported by the text or that misrepresent or seriously exaggerate what should be minor concerns. The writing may ramble or veer away from the task, or it may fall into extended plot summary without links to meaning. These essays show an ability to express basic ideas but demonstrate uncertain control over writing beyond the sentence level. Essays that include significant misreading or unskilled writing should be scored 3.

2–1 These essays compound the weaknesses of the 4–3 essays. They may be unacceptably brief or may badly misinterpret the story. Although they attempt to respond to the task, they do so without clarity, organization, or supporting example. They may be poorly written on several counts and include distracting errors in grammar and mechanics that force rereading. Essays with little coherent discussion of the story should be scored 1.

0 These essays may make no more than a reference to the task.

— These essays are either left blank or are completely off topic.

SCORING GUIDELINES FOR QUESTION 3

9–8 These persuasive essays identify an appropriate novel, play, or epic in which money plays a significant role. They articulate clearly a meaning of the work as a whole and show compellingly the role money plays in it. These essays may be the most successful at exploiting the phrase "or its equivalent" and choose to examine the role played by land or possessions, always seeing them in a role money could play. They explain with precision and apt concrete details from the text how the writer uses money to establish, develop, or explain character or to manipulate plot. They are not without flaw, but they are focused and organized, weaving details from the text into their analysis with skill. They show that the writer reads with perception and has practiced and sophisticated control over the techniques of expressing that perception.

7–6 These essays present a lucid and credible explanation of the impact of money on a clearly stated meaning of the work. The account of that relationship may be more mechanical or less smoothly articulated and the essays less thorough or specific than the top papers, but they demonstrate both an accurate reading of the work and sufficient control over the elements of writing about literature. Essays scored 7 will have stronger textual support for their analysis and, generally, more expertise of expression than those scored 6.

Credits: P. 12, Frank O'Connor, "The Drunkard" from Collected Stories. Copyright © 1981 by Harriet O'Donovan Sheehy, Executrix of the Estate of Frank O'Connor. Reprinted with the permission of Alfred A. Knopf, a division of Random House, Inc. and Lyons & Pande International LLC as agent for the proprietor. P. 14, Sylvia Plath, "Mirror" from CROSSING THE WATER. Copyright © 1960, 1963 by Ted Hughes. Reprinted by permission of HarperCollins Publishers and Faber and Faber, Ltd. P. 16, William Shakespeare, Othello, the Moor of Venice from Shakespeare: The Complete Works, edited by G B Harrison. Copyright 1952 by Harcourt Brace & Company, renewed © 1980 by G. B. Harrison. Reprinted with the permission of Harcourt, Inc. P. 19, James Baldwin, "Sonny's Blues" © 1957 by James Baldwin was originally published in PARTISAN REVIEW. Copyright renewed. Collected in GOING TO MEET THE MAN, published by Vintage Books. (New York: Dial Press, 1965). Reprinted by arrangement with the James Baldwin Estate. P. 23, Countee Cullen, "Yet Do I Marvel" from COLOR. Copyright 1925 by Harper & Brothers, renewed 1953 by Ida M. Cullen. Copyrights held by the Amistad Research Center, Tulane University, administered by Thompson and Thompson, Brooklyn, NY. P. 24, Jhumpa Lahiri, "Interpreter of Maladies" from INTERPRETER OF MALADIES. Copyright © 1999 by Jhumpa Lahiri. Reprinted with the permission of Houghton Mifflin Company. All rights reserved. P. 73, Emily Dickinson, "There is no Frigate like a Book" from THE COMPLETE POEMS OF EMILY DICKINSON, edited by Thomas H. Johnson. Copyright 1951, © 1955, 1979, 1983 by the President and Fellows of Harvard College. Reprinted by permission of the publishers and the Trustees of Amherst College. P. 75, Wilfred Owen, "Dulce et Decorum Est" from THE COMPLETE POEMS AND FRAGMENTS OF WILFRED OWEN, edited by Jon Stallworthy (New York: W. W. Norton & Company, 1984). P. 76, Charles Simic, "Old Soldier" from THE NEW YORKER (December 20, 2004). Copyright © 2004 by Charles Simic. Reprinted with the permission of Charles Simic. P. 85, Richard Connell, "The Most Dangerous Game." Copyright 1924 by Richard Connell, renewed 1952 by Louise Fox Connell. Reprinted by permission of Brandt & Hochman Literary Agents, Inc. P. 88, Tim O'Brien, "The Things They Carried" from THE THINGS THEY CARRIED. Copyright © 1990 by Tim O'Brien. Reprinted by permission of Houghton Mifflin Harcourt Publishing Company. All rights reserved. P. 113, Chinua Achebe, "Civil Peace" from Girls at War. Copyright © 1972, 1973 by Chinua Achebe. Reprinted with the permission of Doubleday, a division of Random House, Inc. and the Emma Sweeney Literary Agency, LLC. P. 118, Philip Larkin, "Aubade" from Collected Poems from Collected Poems, edited by Anthony Thwaite. Copyright © 1988 by The Estate of Philip Larkin. Reprinted with the permission of Farrar, Straus & Giroux, LLC and Faber & Faber, Ltd. P. 120, Molière, "Tartuffe, or The Impostor" from TARTUFFE: COMEDY IN FIVE ACTS, translated by Richard Wilbur. Copyright © 1963, 1962, 1961, and renewed 1991, 1990, 1989 by Richard Wilbur. Reprinted with the permission of Harcourt, Inc. CAUTION: Professionals and amateurs are hereby warned that this translation, being fully protected under the copyright laws of the United States of America, the British Empire, including the Dominion of Canada, and all other countries which are signatories of the Universal Copyright Convention, is subject to royalty. All rights, including professional, amateur, motion picture, recitation, lecturing, public reading, radio broadcasting, and the rights of translation into foreign languages, are strictly reserved. Particular emphasis is laid on the question of readings, permission for which must be secured from the author's agent in writing. Inquiries on professional rights (except amateur) should be addressed to Mr. Gilbert Parker, William Morris Agency, 1325 Avenue of the Americas, New York, NY 10019; inquiries on translation rights should be addressed to Harcourt, Inc. Permissions Department, Orlando, FL 32887-6777. P. 124, Linda Pastan, "Ethics" from WAITING FOR MY LIFE. Copyright © 1981 by Linda Pastan. Used by permission of W. W. Norton & Company, Inc. P. 127, Louise Glück, "Gretel in Darkness" from THE FIRST FOUR BOOKS OF POEMS. Copyright © 1968, 1971, 1972, 1973, 1974, 1975, 1976, 1977, 1978, 1979, 1980, 1995 by Louise Glück. Reprinted by permission of HarperCollins Publishers. P. 128, John Updike, "Oliver's Evolution" from LICKS OF LOVE: SHORT STORIES AND A SEQUEL. Copyright © 2000 by John Updike.